Los Angeles Houses

teNeues

Editor in chief:	Paco Asensio
Editor and texts:	Cristina Montes
Editorial coordination:	Cynthia Reschke
Art director:	Mireia Casanovas Soley
Graphic design and layout:	Soti Mas-Bagà, Pilar Cano
Copy-editing:	Francesc Bombí-Vilaseca, Sabine Würfel
German translation:	Susanne Engler
French translation:	Catherine Reschke
English translation:	Suzanne Wales

Published by teNeues Publishing Group

teNeues Publishing Company
16 West 22nd Street, New York, NY 10010, US
Tel.: 001-212-627-9090, Fax: 001-212-627-9511

teNeues Book Division
Neuer Zollhof 1
40221 Düsseldorf, Germany
Tel.: 0049-(0)211-994597-0, Fax: 0049-(0)211-994597-40

teNeues Publishing UK Ltd.
Aldwych House, 71/91 Aldwych
London WC2B 4HN, UK

www.teneues.com

ISBN:	3-8238-5594-8
Editorial project:	© 2002 **LOFT** Publications

Domènech 9, 2º 2ª
08012 Barcelona, Spain
Tel.: 0034 932 183 099
Fax: 0034 932 370 060

e-mail: loft@loftpublications.com
www.loftpublications.com

Printed by:	Gràfiques Anman. Sabadell, Spain
	September 2002

Bibliografische Information Der Deutschen Bibliothek
Die Deutsche Bibliothek verzeichnet diese Publikation in der Deutschen Nationalbibliografie; detaillierte bibliografische Daten sind im Internet über **http://dnb.ddb.de** aburfbar.

Los Angeles Houses

teNeues

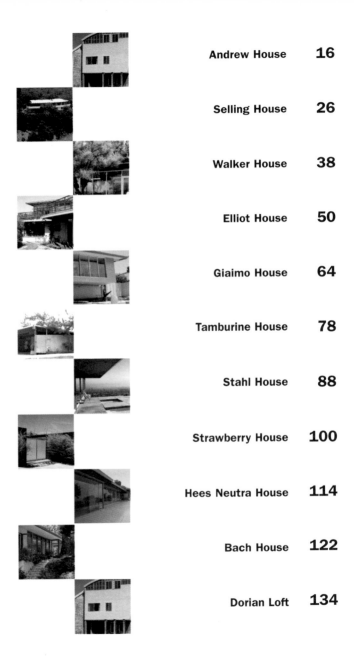

The apocalyptic vision of a future Los Angeles with which Ridley Scott opens one of the most famous science fiction films of all time comes close to the reality of this great metropolis on many fronts. Not true perhaps in the dim, depressing atmosphere it projects of the city, as with the exception of its rainy season, L.A. enjoys a temperate climate where the sun shines all year round, but in other aspects Ridley Scott's Los Angeles was more than visionary. In "Blade Runner", this chaotic city on the Californian coastline is a seething with anonymous beings with individual characters in an immense Tower of Babel of diverse languages and street patter dialects. This image that the director gave us in 1982 is still true at the beginning of the 21st century.

The city of Los Angeles, like all major cities, is unique and it is precisely this mix of cultures, races and individual styles which irremediably converts it into an example of the future metropolis.

'Melting pot' is the best way to define this city whose original name, "El Pueblo de Nuestra Señora Reina de los Ángeles" (the Village of Our Lady, Queen of the Angels), was shortened for obvious reasons.

It is the largest city in California and the second largest in all of the United States. What makes it different from the majority of other cities is that it has no distinct urban centre. Instead, dozens of individual communities are joined together by a complex series of roads and freeways. Every one of these communities is different with its own unique, personal character. Together they form the intricate network that is known as Los Angeles.

Diversity seeps from its every pore. Everything here is excessive, exuberant, over-the-top and larger-than-life. Its contrasts enrich and its diversity makes it place full of nuance, colour and a zest for life. Here lies the charm of this urban conglomeration: a variety of moods and atmospheres that lures you away from the centre and into the suburbs.

A diversity that is also reflected (and rightly so) in its architecture and the interiors of its homes. Stylistic richness is abundant and its fruitful aesthetic, decorative and visual, generous and imaginative.

Victorian-style homes located near indescribably dilapidated areas, the commercial architecture that marked the city in the 1920s living side by side with contemporary buildings, low-rent housing nestled between the condos of young urban professionals and hectare upon hectare of gardens and museums.

Los Angeles is a city of contrasts. A place where run-down, working class neighbourhoods are swamped by the grand mansions of Hollywood's film stars and the hubbub of the downtown commercial area.

Despite its reputation having being built upon the 'dream' world of Hollywood, the mythic image that the city offers is often in decay when you get to know the territory and come fact to face with its often-cruel reality. With every step the city shows you its multiple personalities, some of them, a rude awakening.

If Hollywood is in charge of showing its distorted image of the real world, the popular Venice Beach acts as a showcase for the lifestyle of its inhabitants: its long boulevard acts as a catwalk where people from all walks of life are on parade.

The pages of L.A. Houses display this diversity and multiculturalism through the city's architecture. The book is an impressive col-

lection of the most attractive, daring, distinctive and simply breathtaking interiors of Los Angeles by well-known architects and decorators. Names such as Richard Neutra, Eric Owen Moss, Pierre Koenig, Michael B. Lehrer, Paul Murdoch, Austin Ayers, Arata Isozaki, J. Frank Fitzgibbons and Frank O. Gehry (just to name a few) have all been inspired by L.A.'s pluralism and diversification. The fruit of this can be seen the generous mansions, luxury apartments, dream homes and residences that embrace their natural surroundings; dwellings that display a wide range of styles and a thought-provoking eclecticism. Interiors that reflect the aesthetic richness of a city that surprises travellers as soon as they arrive. Arriving in Los Angeles by air is an unforgettable experience: an immense urban sprawl, both brave and arrogant, unfolds before your eyes. It is a place where, just sometimes, even the most far-flung dreams really do come true.

Die apokalyptische Vision des Los Angeles der Zukunft, mit der Ridley Scott einen der erfolgreichsten Sciencefictionfilme eröffnete, ist der Realität dieser großen Metropole in vielen Aspekten sehr ähnlich. Vielleicht entspricht die beklemmende, düstere und deprimierende Atmosphäre des Films nicht ganz der Wirklichkeit, da in dieser Stadt doch meist die Sonne scheint und das ganze Jahr über eine warme, angenehme Temperatur herrscht (abgesehen von den Wochen, in denen es viel regnet). Dennoch ist das Bild, das Ridley Scott zeichnete, in vielen Aspekten nicht nur eine bloße Vision. In „Blade Runner" ist die chaotische Stadt an der kalifornischen Küste ein Gewimmel anonymer Wesen, die ihre Besonderheiten mit sich herumschleppen, eine Art Turm von Babylon, in dem alle Sprachen und Jargons zu finden sind. In dieser Vision, die der Regisseur im Jahr 1982 entwarf, sind weiterhin zahlreiche Ähnlichkeiten mit dem Los Angeles zu Beginn des 21. Jh. zu finden. Allerdings ist nicht alles so, wie der Film es darstellte.

Die Stadt Los Angeles ist wie alle Großstädte einzigartig. Das Gemisch aus Kulturen, Ethnien und Stilen, die hier zusammentreffen und zusammen leben, machen zwangsläufig ein Beispiel für die Megalopolis der Zukunft aus der Stadt.

‚Schmelztiegel' ist das Wort, das diese Stadt, die ursprünglich „El Pueblo de Nuestra Seño-ra Reina de los Ángeles" (das Dorf unserer Jungfrau, Königin der Engel) hieß, am besten definiert. Aus verständlichen Gründen setzte sich eine Kurzform des Namens durch.

L.A. ist die größte Stadt Kaliforniens und die zweitgrößte der USA, und im Gegensatz zu den meisten Städten gibt es in L.A. kein definiertes Stadtzentrum. Es handelt sich vielmehr um eine Reihe individueller Gemeinden, die durch ein komplexes Straßen- und Autobahnnetz miteinander verbunden sind. Jede Gemeinde ist anders und hat ihren einzigartigen, persönlichen Charakter, und alle zusammen formen diesen verflochtenen Komplex, der als Los Angeles bezeichnet wird.

Die Pluralität fließt durch alle Adern der Stadt. Alles in ihr ist übermäßig, gewaltig, anmaßend und riesig. Die Gegensätze bereichern die Stadt und die Vielfalt macht sie zu einem Ort voller verschiedener Aspekte und Farben. Ein überaus lebendiges Großstadtkonglomerat, dessen Zauber die Menschen gefangen nimmt, mit einer Vielzahl verschiedener Umgebungen, die noch unterschiedlicher werden, je weiter man sich vom Zentrum entfernt und in die Vorstädte eindringt.

Diese Vielfältigkeit spiegelt sich natürlich auch in der Architektur und Innendekoration der Häuser und Wohnungen wider. Der stilistische Reichtum und die ästhetische Fruchtbarkeit sind überwältigend. Phantasievolle, großzügige und einfallsreiche Dekoration sind überall zu finden.

So gibt es Häuser im viktorianischen Stil in unbeschreiblich dekadenten Umgebungen; die kommerzielle Architektur, die den Stil der Stadt in den zwanziger Jahren kennzeichnete, teilt sich den Raum mit zeitgenössischen Gebäuden; billige Mietshäusern stehen Seite an Seite mit Gebäuden, die von wohlhabenden jungen Menschen bewohnt werden, und dazwischen befinden sich großzügig angelegte, riesige Gärten und Museen.

L. A. ist die Stadt der Gegensätze, der Ort, an dem sich die armseligsten Viertel zwischen den prächtigen Villen der Hollywoodstars und dem geschäftlichen Treiben aufzulösen scheinen.

Und das, obwohl die Stadt ihren Ruhm der irrealen Welt des Zelluloid verdankt. Doch dieser fast mythische Ruf zerbröckelt oft, wenn man die Stadt und ihre brutale Realität wirklich kennen lernt. Los Angeles zeigt bei jedem Schritt seine vielen, teilweise völlig unbekannten Gesichter.

Hollywood hat die Aufgabe übernommen, der Welt ein verzerrtes Bild der Realität zu übermitteln und der berühmte Strand Venice Beach fasst den Lebensstil der Bewohner von L.A. zusammen. Seine Strandpromenade ist ein großer Laufsteg, auf dem sich alle möglichen Typen von Menschen verschiedenen Standes und Herkunft zur Schau stellen.

L.A. Houses zeigt diese große Vielfalt und Multikulturalität auf seinen Seiten in Form architektonischer Entwürfe. Der Band beinhaltet eine beachtliche Zusammenstellung der attraktivsten, gewagtesten, schönsten und einzigartigsten Innendekorationen der Stadt, die von bekannten Architekten und Innenarchitekten entworfen wurden. Richard Neutra, Eric Owen Moss, Pierre Koenig, Michael B. Lehrer, Paul Murdoch, Austin Ayers, Arata Isozaki, J. Frank Fitzgibbons oder Frank O. Gehry sind nur einige der Architekten und Innenarchitekten, die sich von der Mannigfaltigkeit und Vermischung, die in der ganzen Stadt zu finden ist, inspirieren ließen und sie in großzügige Villen, luxuriöse Appartements, traumhafte Wohnstätten oder offene Parklandschaften umsetzten, die von einer Vielfalt von Stilen und einem ansprechenden Eklektizismus geprägt sind. Wohnlandschaften, die den ästhetischen Reichtum der Stadt widerspiegeln, und den Reisenden vom ersten Augenblick an faszinieren. Per Flugzeug in Los Angeles anzukommen ist ein unvergessliches Erlebnis. Vor dem Besucher erstreckt sich eine unendliche Stadt, die sich wagemutig und hochmütig seinen Blicken darbietet. Sie ist zweifelsohne das Paradigma der Stadt der Zukunft, ein Ort, an dem manchmal die gewagtesten Träume in Erfüllung gehen.

La vision apocalyptique d'un future Los Angeles avec laquelle Ridley Scott commence l'un des films de science fiction les plus célèbres du monde, est proche de la réalité pour cette métropole aux mille facettes. Moins vrai de par l'atmosphère triste et déprimente, car à l'exception de la saison pluvieuse, L.A. jouit d'un climat tempéré et le soleil y brille toute l'année, mais de par d'autres aspects, le Los Angeles de Ridley Scott était plus que visionnaire. Dans « Blade Runner », cette cité chaotique sur la côte californienne, grouille d'êtres anonymes de charatères individuels, dans une immense Tour de Babel de langages divers et de dialectes baratinants de la rue. Cette image qui nous en est donnée en 1982 est encore valable au début du 21ème siècle.

La ville de Los Angeles, comme toute autre grande ville, est unique et c'est précisément ce mélange de cultures, de races et de styles individuels qui en font un exemple des métropoles futures.

« Tout dans le même pot » est la meilleure façon de définir cette ville dont le nom d'origin « El Pueblo de Nuestra Señora Reina de los Ángeles » (le Village de Notre Dame Reine des Anges), fût abrégé pour d'évidentes raisons.

C'est la ville la plus grande de Californie et la 2ème de tout les États-Unis. Ce qui la différencie de la majorité des autres villes est qu'elle ne possède pas de centre urbain proprement dit, mais par contre une douzaine de communautés reliées entre elles par un vaste réseau de routes et autoroutes. Chacune de ces communauté a son caractère propre. Réunies, elles forment l'ensemble très complexe connu sous le nom de Los Angeles.

La diversité sort de chacun de ses pores. Tout ici est excessif, exubérant, mieux et plus grand que partout ailleurs. Ses contrastes l'enrichissent et sa diversité en font un endroit plein de nuances et de couleurs lui donnant son cachet particulier. C'est là que se trouve le charme de cette agglomération : Un changement perpétuel d'humeurs et d'atmosphères vous attire hors du centre, dans la banlieue.

Une diversité également reflétée, heureusement, dans son architecture ainsi qu'à l'intérieur de ses maisons. La richesse stylistique est abondante et d'une estétique très visuelle, décorative généreuse et imaginative.

Des villas de style Victorien aux abords de quartiers complètements délabrés, une architecture marquante des années 1920, côtoyant des bâtiments contemporains, des logements à loyers modérés situés entre les appartements haut-standing de jeunes cadres, tout cela entouré de jardins et de musées à n'en plus finir.

Los Angeles est une ville pleine de contrastes. Un lieu également où les quartiers ouvriers délabré viennent remplacés par les immenses demeures des Stars hollywoodiennes et l'expension des zones commerciales du centre ville.

Malgré sa réputation d'avoir été construite sur le monde de rêve de Hollywood l'image mythique de cette cité se dégrade lorsqu'on fait connaîssance avec ce territoire et que l'on est confronté à une réalité souvent cruelle. A chaque pas la ville vous montre ses multiples facettes dont quelques unes vous ramènent brutalement à la réalité.

Si Hollywood est responsable de cette image déformée de la réalité, la plage de Venice, elle, joue un rôle de vitrine où l'on peut voire le style de vie de ses habitants : Ses longs boulevards ressemblent à une scène où défilent des gens de toute les conditions sociales.

Les pages du « L.A. Houses » montrent cette diversité et cet aspect multiculturel à travers l'architecture de la ville ce livre est un recueil impressionant des intérieurs les plus beaux, les plus audacieux et tout simplement les plus sensationnels de Los Angeles, qui ont été conçû par des architectes et des décorateurs renommés. Ce sont pour en nommer quelques un : Richard Neutra, Eric Owen Moss, Pierre Koenig, Michael B. Lehrer, Paul Murdoch, Austin Ayers, Arata Isozaki, J. Frank Fitzgibbons et Frank O. Gehry. Tous ont été inspirés par le pluralisme et la diversité de L.A. On le découvre à la vue de ces impressionnantes maisons, de ces appartements luxueux, de ces résidences de rêve situées dans un cadre fantastique et un environnement naturel; des habitations montrant une grande gamme de styles et d'un éclectisme invitant à la réflexion. Des intérieurs reflètant la richesse esthétique d'une ville qui surprend le visiteur aussitôt qu'il débarque. Arriver à Los Angeles par avion est une expérience inoubliable : Une cité gigantesque brave et arrogante à la fois s'étend sous vous yeux. C'est un endroit où même les rêves les plus fous peuvent parfois devenir réalité.

La apocalíptica visión de Los Ángeles del futuro con la que Ridley Scott abría una de las películas más aplaudidas del género de ciencia ficción se acerca, en numerosos aspectos, a la realidad de esta gran metrópolis. Puede que la atmósfera tétrica, oscura y deprimente que proponía el filme no se corresponda con la realidad, ya que el sol acostumbra a brillar y las temperaturas son cálidas y agradables casi todo el año (descartando una determinada época de lluvias), pero en otros aspectos la definición de Ridley Scott era más que visionaria. En "Blade Runner", la caótica ciudad de la costa californiana es un hervidero de seres anónimos que pasean su singularidad y una inmensa Torre de Babel en la que tienen cabida todas las lenguas y jergas. Esa imagen que el cineasta proponía en 1982 sigue manteniendo –salvando las distancias, por supuesto– numerosas similitudes con Los Ángeles del siglo XXI.

La ciudad de Los Ángeles es, como todas las urbes, única, pero es precisamente esta amalgama de culturas, etnias y estilos que en ella conviven lo que la convierte irremediablemente en un ejemplo de megalópolis del futuro.

Crisol sería la palabra que mejor podría definir a esta ciudad, cuya denominación original era El Pueblo de Nuestra Señora Reina de los Ángeles, aunque se adoptó una versión reducida del nombre.

Se trata de la ciudad más grande de California y la segunda más grande de todo Estados Unidos, y, a diferencia de la mayoría, Los Ángeles no tiene un centro urbano distintivo. Más bien podría hablarse de una colección de comunidades individuales enlazadas unas con otras por una compleja red de autopistas y viales. Cada comunidad es diferente y ofrece un carácter único y personal; todas juntas forman ese complejo entramado denominado Los Ángeles.

La pluralidad fluye por los poros de su piel. En ella todo es excesivo, exuberante, descarado, desmesurado. Los contrastes la enriquecen y la diversidad la convierte en un lugar lleno de matices, de color y repleto de vida. Ese es el encanto de esta conglomerada urbe. Una diversidad de ambientes que se acentúa a medida que uno se aleja del centro y se dirige a los suburbios.

Esta pluralidad también tiene su reflejo, cómo no, en su arquitectura y los interiores de las viviendas. La riqueza estilística es abundante y la fecundidad estética, decorativa y visual generosa e imaginativa.

Casas de estilo victoriano rodeadas de zonas de indescriptible deterioro; la arquitectura comercial, que marcó el estilo de la ciudad en los años 20, convive con edificaciones contemporáneas; viviendas de alquileres baratos codo con codo con espacios habitados por jóvenes acomodados y con generosas hectáreas de jardines y museos.

L.A. es la ciudad de los contrastes, el lugar en el que las zonas más deprimidas se diluyen ante las generosas mansiones de las estrellas de Hollywood y el bullicio comercial.

A pesar de haberse construido su reputación sobre el encanto del mundo irreal del celuloide, la imagen mítica que ofrece la urbe se desmorona, en ocasiones, cuando se conoce a fondo su territorio y su cruda realidad. A cada paso la ciudad muestra sus múltiples caras, algunas de ellas grandes desconocidas.

Si Hollywood se ha encargado de lanzar al mundo una imagen distorsionada de la realidad, la conocida playa de Venice Beach resume el estilo de vida de sus habitantes: su paseo marítimo es una gran pasarela por la que desfila gente de todo tipo, condición y procedencia.

"L.A. Houses" recoge en sus páginas toda esa diversidad y multiculturalidad mediante los proyectos arquitectónicos que en él aparecen. Este volumen es una imponente recopilación de los interiores más atractivos, atrevidos, bellos y singulares de Los Ángeles firmados por reconocidos arquitectos y decoradores. Profesionales de la talla de Richard Neutra, Eric Owen Moss, Pierre Koenig, Michael B. Lehrer, Paul Murdoch, Austin Ayers, Rodney Walker, John Lautner, Dean Nota o Frank O. Gehry, por citar sólo algunos, que se han inspirado en ese mestizaje que recorre esta gran ciudad y lo han materializado en generosas mansiones, lujosos apartamentos, residencias de ensueño o espacios abiertos al paisaje que muestran una amplia variedad de estilos además de un sugerente eclecticismo. Unos interiores que reflejan la riqueza estética de una ciudad que sorprende al viajero ya desde su llegada. Arribar a Los Ángeles en avión resulta toda una experiencia: uno se encuentra con una inmensa extensión urbana que se muestra osada y altanera ante sus ojos. Ella es, sin duda, el paradigma de ciudad del futuro. Un lugar en el que, en ocasiones, los sueños más atrevidos se ven recompensados.

Ingenious architectural solutions, volumes that combine straight lines with rounded contours to give an ultimately and restrained appearance: these are the features of this dwelling that in the end forms part of its surroundings. The interior distribution acts as a stage in which the designer furnishings, as the architecture itself, are the main characters. This elegant, hospitable home can only be truly appreciated by taking in all its details including the harmonious blend of different tendencies and styles. A lesson in intelligent decoration that gives fruit to an interior as balanced as it is functional.

Einfallsreiche architektonische Lösungen, welche die zurückhaltenden, kompakten Formen und die geraden Linien mit einigen runden Umrissen kombinieren. So sieht dieses Wohnhaus aus, das perfekt an seiner Umgebung teilhat. Die Raumaufteilung lässt eine Bühne entstehen, auf der die Designermöbel ebenso wie die Architektur zu den Hauptdarstellern des Hauses werden. Um dieses freundliche und elegante Wohnambiente, in dem verschiedene Trends und Stilrichtungen harmonisch kombiniert werden, wirklich zu genießen, sollte man auf alle Details achten. Eine Lektion in intelligenter Innenarchitektur mit ebenso ausgeglichenen wie funktionellen Wohnräumen.

Andrew House

Architect: **SITI Studio Architects** Photos: © **Ricardo Labougle**

17

Grâce à des solutions architecturales pleines d'idées combinant des formes réservées et compactes à des lignes droites ayant quelques arrondis, cette maison fait partie intégrale de son environnement. La répartition des pièces en font une scène sur laquelle le design des meubles ainsi que l'architecture en sont les vedettes. Pour apprécier l'atmosphère acceuillante et élégante dans laquelle divers styles et tendances sont harmonieusement combinés, il est nécessaire de faire attention à chaque détail. Une leçon d'architecture d'intérieur intélligente, où l'espace habitable est aussi équilibré que fonctionnel.

Ingeniosas soluciones arquitectónicas, un aspecto contenido y compacto y volúmenes que combinan las líneas rectas con algunos contornos redondeados. Así es esta vivienda que participa del entorno que la envuelve. La distribución interior se plantea como un escenario en el que el mobiliario de diseño se convierte, al igual que la arquitectura, en el gran protagonista de la vivienda. Reparar en todos los detalles es la mejor manera de disfrutar de este espacio acogedor y elegante en el que diferentes tendencias y estilos conviven sin estridencias. Una lección de interiorismo inteligente que configura unos ambientes tan equilibrados como funcionales.

The recognizable forms that make up this project of John Lautner's (in his work nothing is left to chance) belong to a home constructed in 1982 on the West Coast of Los Angeles. Situated on a privileged plot of land with panoramic views, the house opens itself up to the natural splendour outside and manages to effortlessly dissolve the partition between exterior and interior. Four years ago the home was restored and re-defined, new spaces were created and interior features changed. The result: a classic of modern architecture that boldly confronts the future.

Die für die Arbeiten von John Lautner typischen Formen, an dessen Architektur nichts willkürlich oder zufällig ist, sind deutlich an diesem 1982 erbauten Wohnhaus an der Westküste von L.A. erkennbar. Das Haus liegt in einer wundervollen Umgebung mit einer beeindruckenden Aussicht und es öffnet sich mit all seiner Pracht nach außen. Die Grenzen zwischen innen und außen verschwimmen auf natürliche Weise. Vor ungefähr vier Jahren wurde das Haus renoviert, neu definiert, die Räume wurden verändert und es kamen neue hinzu. Das Ergebnis ist ein Klassiker der modernen Architektur, der sich ohne Komplexe der Zukunft stellen kann.

Selling House

Architect: **John Lautner** Reformation: **Duncan Nicholson**
Interior design: **Harriet Selling** Photos: © **Ricardo Labougle**

Cette maison située sur la côte, à l'ouest de Los Angeles, fût construite en 1982. On y trouve les formes typiques à l'architecture et au travail de John Lautner. Rien n'est laissé au hasard. Cette maison qui est dans un environnement magnifique, jouit d'une vue impressionnante et s'ouvre dans toute sa splendeur sur l'extérieur. Les frontières entre l'intérieur et l'extérieur s'estompent de façon naturelle. Elle a été rénovée il y a quatre ans. On lui donnat un nouveau caractère en transformant certaines pièces et en ajoutant d'autres. Le résultat est un classique de l'architecture moderne pouvant affronter l'avenir sans aucun complexe.

Las reconocibles formas que definen el trabajo de John Lautner –en su arquitectura nada es arbitrario o accidental– se manifiestan en esta vivienda construida en 1982 en la costa oeste de Los Ángeles. Situada en un enclave privilegiado desde el cual es posible disfrutar de las impresionantes panorámicas del entorno, la casa se abre al exterior con todo su esplendor diluyendo las fronteras entre interior y exterior de forma natural. Hace cuatro años una intervención permitió restaurar, redefinir y crear nuevos espacios a la vez que cambió la fisonomía de los interiores. El resultado: un clásico de la arquitectura moderna que se enfrenta sin complejos al futuro.

An unusual setting with a striking use of geometry and volumes carried out in accordance to the rationalist creed are the calling card of this home designed by Rodney Walker in 1951. As in other projects of the architect, the edifice transmits a longing for experimentation with materials, a marked tendency for modernist structure and an objective of creating an innovative aesthetic whist still retaining functionality. The result is a space that is still thoroughly contemporary more than 50 years after its construction. Its calculated interiors only serve to accentuate the home's attractive and timeless architectural lines.

Die einzigartige Lage dieses Hauses und die beeindruckenden geometrischen, vom Rationalismus beeinflussten Formen sind die Visitenkarte dieses Hauses, das Rodney Walker 1951 erbaute. Wie auch bei anderen Werken dieses Architekten, drückt das Gebäude sein Verlangen danach aus, mit Materialien zu experimentieren. Ohne die Funktionalität außer Acht zu lassen, verwendete er moderne Strukturen und erreichte so eine innovative Ästhetik. Ergebnis dieser Bemühungen ist ein Gebäude, das zwar schon über 50 Jahre alt, aber immer noch extrem modern ist. Die sorgfältige Aufteilung der Räume betont die attraktiven und zeitlosen architektonischen Linien.

Walker House

Architect: **Rodney Walker** Photos: © **Ricardo Labougle**

39

Son emplacement exceptionnel ainsi que ses formes géométriques imposantes influencées par un certain rationalisme, sont la carte de visite de cette maison, construite en 1951 par Rodney Walker. De même que dans d'autre œuvres de cet architecte, ce bâtiment exprime son désir d'expérimenter avec divers matériaux. Sans perdre de vue la fonctionalité, il utilisat des structures modernes et obtint de cette façon un esthétisme inovatif. Le résultat de ses efforts est une construction qui bien que datant de 50 ans déjà, est encore très moderne. La soigneuse répartition des pièces souligne les lignes architecturales classiques et plaisantes.

La singular ubicación de la casa y los geométricos y contundentes volúmenes –que se rigen por el credo racionalista– son la mejor carta de presentación de esta vivienda proyectada por Rodney Walker en 1951. Al igual que ocurre con otros trabajos del arquitecto, la construcción transmite ese ansia de experimentación con los materiales, una marcada decantación por las estructuras modernas y la intención de lograr una estética innovadora sin perder la funcionalidad. El resultado es un espacio extremadamente moderno a pesar de contar con más de 50 años. La cuidada resolución de los interiores no hace más que acentuar unas atractivas y atemporales líneas arquitectónicas.

Generous open spaces that are vital and full of light define this home designed by the architect Austin Ayers in 1946. The surrounding countryside and privileged position of the plot allows nature to become a backdrop for a project of marked, geometric rationalist lines executed in brick, metallic profiles and glass. This suggestive and refined selection of materials fuses exterior and interior in some areas of the home and the sober decoration in the interior only serves to enhance the beauty of its architectural forms.

Großzügige, helle, lebendige und offene Räume definieren dieses Haus, das 1946 von dem Architekten Austin Ayers entworfen wurde. Die bezaubernde Umgebung und die besonders schöne Lage des Gebäudes machen aus der Landschaft einen Hintergrund, vor dem sich die rationalistischen und geometrischen Linien aus Ziegelstein, Metallprofilen und Glas deutlich abheben. Durch die ansprechende und treffsichere Auswahl der Materialien erreichte der Architekt, dass in einigen Bereichen des Hauses die Verbindung zwischen innen und außen absolut ist, und die zurückhaltende Dekoration der Innenräume unterstreicht die architektonische Schönheit der Formen zusätzlich.

Elliot House

Architect: **Austin Ayers**   Interior design: **Alexandra Angle (Aqua Vitae Design)**

Photos: © **Ricardo Labougle**

51

Des pièces ouvertes, généreuses, claires et vivantes définissent cette maison, construite en 1946 par Austin Ayers. Le cadre enchanteur et la situation très attrayante de ce bâtiment font du paysage une coulisse de laquelle les lignes rationelles et géométriques en brique, métal et verre se distinguent particulièrement. L'architecte obtient grâce à son choix juste et plaisant des matériaux, que la liaison entre certains espaces intérieurs et extérieurs s'estompe, et la décoration résevée des lieux ne fait que souligner la beauté architecturale des formes.

Espacios generosos, iluminados, vitales y abiertos definen a esta vivienda proyectada en 1946 por el arquitecto Austin Ayers. El envolvente paisaje que la rodea y la privilegiada situación de su enclave consiguen que la natauraleza se convierta en el telón de fondo sobre el que destacan unas marcadas líneas racionalistas y geométricas levantadas en ladrillo, perfiles de metálicos y cristal. La sugerente y acertada elección de materiales permite que la conexión entre interior y exterior sea absoluta en algunas áreas de la vivienda y la sobria decoración de las estancias se encarga de potenciar la belleza arquitectónica de sus formas.

With a genuinely American air and the true stylistic essence of the fifties, this home, constructed in 1953 by the architect Edward Fickett, is a clear example of how it is possible to design a building that stands the test of time and the tyranny of trends. The contents and symmetric layout of its façade are a tell-tale sign of what's inside: a fresh, vital and hugely expressive interior abundant in furnishings that have become even more appreciated over the years and now form a part of the history of contemporary design. A dwelling brimming with personality that is marked by eclecticism and a daring use of colours.

Dieses Haus im echt amerikanischen Stil, durchdrungen von der Essenz der fünfziger Jahre, wurde von dem Architekten Edward Fickett im Jahr 1953 erbaut. Es ist ein deutliches Beispiel für zeitloses Bauen, das sich der Tyrannei der Mode nicht unterwirft. Die symmetrischen Linien der Fassade deuten bereits auf die lebendigen und ausdrucksvollen Räume im Inneren hin, voller erstaunlicher Möbel, die einen Teil der Geschichte des zeitgenössischen Designs bilden und so weder unmodern noch vergessen wurden. Räume mit betontem Eigencharakter, der sich durch seinen Eklektizismus und die gewagten Farbkombinationen auszeichnet.

Giaimo House

Architect: **Edward Fickett** Photos: © **Ricardo Labougle**

65

Cette maison d'un style typiquement américain est imprégnée du flair des années 50. Elle fût construite 1953 par l'architecte Edward Fickett. C'est l'exemple net d'une construction classique qui ne se soumet pas aux influences de la mode. Les lignes symmétriques de la façade laissent supposer de la vitalité et de l'expression de l'aménagement intérieur, meublé d'éléments étonnants qui constituent une partie de l'histoire du design contemporain et qui, de ce fait, ne sont ni démodés ni tombés dans l'oubli. Les différentes pièces ont une expression particulière qui se caractérise de par leur éclectisme et des combinaisons de couleurs très osées.

Con un sabor genuinamente americano e impregnada de la esencia y el estilo de los años 50, esta vivienda –construida en 1953 por el arquitecto Edward Fickett– es un claro ejemplo de cómo es posible edificar una construcción para la que no existe el paso del tiempo ni la tiranía de las modas. Los contenidos y simétricos trazos de su fachada son el presagio de unos interiores frescos, vitales y rabiosamente expresivos, llenos de reconocidas piezas de mobiliario que lejos de quedar desfasadas y relegadas al olvido se han revalorizado y han pasado a formar parte de la historia del diseño contemporáneo. Un espacio lleno de personalidad marcado por el eclectisimo y las atrevidas combinaciones cromáticas.

Marked by the topographic conditions of its location, this home, a project of Richard Dorman in 1958, was inspired by contrasts when it came to the application of its stylistic resources and architectural strategy. A subtle interplay of opposites (open-closed, light-shade, light-solid etc.) were used in the interior where a cool and transparent atmosphere is interchanged with a warm and welcoming one by fusing together different materials and textures. The result is an attractive composition in which flat surfaces and volumes interact, creating an evocative edifice, which is seemingly not tainted by the passing of time nor trends.

Dieses Haus, 1958 von Richard Dorman entworfen, wurde von den topografischen Bedingungen der Umgebung bestimmt. Bei der Umsetzung stilistischer Mittel ließ sich der Architekt von Gegensätzen inspirieren (offen–geschlossen, Licht–Schatten, Leichtigkeit–Festigkeit). Sie dominieren die Räume, in denen eine kalte und transparente Atmosphäre herrscht, die wiederum durch die Fusion verschiedener Materialien warm und einladend wird. Das Ergebnis ist eine attraktive Mischung aus Ebenen und Formen, die kombiniert werden und ein beeindruckendes Gebäude entstehen lassen, das sich von dem Lauf der Zeit und der Mode nicht beeindrucken lässt.

Tamburine House

Architect: **Richard Dorman** Photos: © **Peter Polster**

79

Cette maison conçue en 1958 par Richard Dorman, est marquée par les conditions topographiques de l'enclave qu'elle occupe. Dorman s'inspira des contrastes lorsqu'il dû appliquer les resources stylistiques et architecturales requisent. Le jeu subtil des contraires (ouvert-fermé, ombre-lumière, légèreté-solidité) détermine l'agencement de l'intérieur, où une atmosphère froide et transparente domine. Elle se réchauffe et devient accueillante grâce à la fusion des divers matériaux et textures. Le résultat est attrayant grâce à l'interaction des niveaux et des volumes qui crée un édifice pouvant résister aux tendances de la mode et au temps qui passe.

Marcada por las condiciones topográficas del enclave en el que se ubica, esta vivienda proyectada por Richard Dorman en 1958 se inspira en los contrastes a la hora de aplicar los recursos estilísticos y las soluciones arquitectónicas. El sutil juego de oposiciones (abierto-cerrado, luz-sombra, ligereza-solidez...) se encarga de organizar unos interiores dominados por una atmósfera fría y transparente que se torna cálida y acogedora al fusionar diferentes materiales y texturas. El resultado es una atractiva composición en la que planos y volúmenes interaccionan creando una sugerente edificación a la que parece no afectarle el paso del tiempo y las modas.

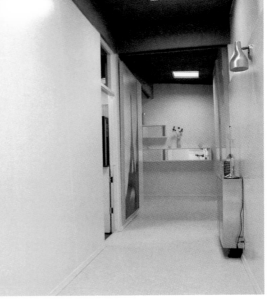

An absolute minimalism seeps through every corner of the home-studio constructed in 1960 by Pierre Koenig. Here the architect employed some of the features that best defined his work: ethereal volumes in steel, evocative geometric profiles, lineal layouts and a sublime austerity. Visually, the connection between the exterior and interior is constant, as the surroundings also form a part of the interior decoration. This is an inspired home full of ingenious that makes us look at architecture in a different way. After more than 40 years, it still remains utterly modern.

Jeder Winkel dieses Wohnhauses/Ateliers, das 1960 von Pierre Koenig entworfen wurde, ist von absoluter, minimalistischer Einfachheit geprägt. Der Architekt verwendete erneut eine der Formeln, die seine Arbeit am besten definieren: ätherische Volumen aus Stahl, fantasieanregende, geometrische Profile, lineare Umrisse und eine erhabene Nüchternheit. Die visuelle Kommunikation zwischen innen und außen wird nicht unterbrochen, deshalb ist die Landschaft ein weiteres Dekorationselement der Räume. Dieses Haus voller Inspiration und Erfindungsgeist stellt eine neue Vision des Architekturverständnisses dar. Ein sehr avantgardistisches Wohnambiente, das, obwohl es schon über vierzig Jahre alt ist, nichts von seiner Aktualität eingebüßt hat.

Stahl House

Architect: **Pierre Koenig** Photos: © **Ricardo Labougle**

89

Chaque recoin de cette maison/atelier conçue en 1960 par Pierre Koenig, est d'un minimalisme et d'une simplicité absolue. Il emploie les formules qui définissent le mieux son travail : volumes d'acier volatils, profiles géométriques stimulant la fantaisie, contours précis et sobriété noble. Il n'y a pas de coupure visuelle entre l'intérieur et l'extérieur. Le paysage devient un élément de décoration supplémentaire. Cette maison pleine d'inspiration et d'esprit innovatif représente une nouvelle vision de la compréhension architecturale, et émet une atmosphère avangardiste. Bien qu'elle existe depuis quarante ans, elle n'a rien perdu de son actualité.

Una absoluta simplicidad minimalista tiñe cada uno de los rincones de esta vivienda estudio proyectada en 1960 por Pierre Koenig. El arquitecto vuelve a emplear algunas de las fórmulas que mejor definen su trabajo: etéreos volúmenes de acero, sugerentes perfiles geométricos, trazos lineales y una sublime austeridad. Visualmente la comunicación entre interior y exterior es constante, por lo que el paisaje participa como un elemento más en la decoración de los espacios. Una casa inspirada y llena de ingenio que plantea otra visión de entender y concebir la arquitectura. Un espacio tremendamente vanguardista a pesar de tener más de cuarenta años de existencia.

This 1963 house is rich in contrasts and with a distinct personal style way that goes far beyond mere fleets of fashion. The stylistic and constructive solutions employed here act as a backdrop for its avant-guard yet timeless furnishings (most of the pieces are one-off), all rigorously selected. Its generous open spaces—bathed in light and always connected to the exterior surrounds—have been laid out with enlightened precision. The result is a calming, functional and welcoming interior in which sobriety and an abundance of architectural geometry are the outstanding features.

Dieses ursprünglich aus dem Jahr 1963 stammende Gebäude ist voller Kontraste und in einem ausgeprägten, eigenen Stil gehalten, der nicht der Vergänglichkeit der Mode unterliegt. Die stilistischen Mittel und die konstruktiven Lösungen werden zum Hintergrund für sorgfältig ausgewählte zeitlose Avantgardemöbel, die meisten davon Originale. Die großzügigen, offenen, in Licht gebadeten Räume sind meisterhaft organisiert und stehen in konstanter Kommunikation mit dem Äußeren. Das Ergebnis sind ruhige, funktionelle und behagliche Räume, deren klaren und nüchternen architektonischen Linien zu den wahren Hauptdarstellern werden.

Strawberry House

Architect: **D. Wallace Benton & Donald G. PRK Architects**
Photos: © **Ricardo Labougle**   Artwork: **Lutz Wessman**

101

Cette maison construite en 1963, est riche en contrastes et a un style propre très marqué, bien au-delà de toutes les modes passagères. Les solutions stylistiques et de construction employées ici servent de toile de fond à un ameublement d'avant-garde, intemporel (la pluspart sont des pièces uniques), soigneusement sélectionné. Les espaces ouverts, généreux, baignés de lumière et en communication constante avec l'extérieur ont été conçu avec beaucoup d'habileté. Le résultat est un intérieur calme, fonctionnel et accueillant, dans lequel la sobriété et les lignes architecturales contondantes en deviennent les vrais protagonistes.

Esta edificación, cuya estructura original data de 1963, es una vivienda rica en contrastes y con un marcado estilo propio alejado de las modas pasajeras. Los recursos estilísticos y el repertorio de soluciones constructivas que emplea se convierten en telón de fondo de un mobiliario vanguardista y atemporal (la mayoría de piezas son originales) cuidadosamente seleccionado. Los generosos espacios abiertos –bañados de luz y constantemente comunicados con el exterior– se organizan con exquisito acierto. El resultado son unos interiores sosegados, funcionales y acogedores en los que la sobriedad y contundencia de las líneas arquitectónicas se convierten en las verdaderas protagonistas.

The relationship between man and nature is constant in the work of Richard Neutra, one of the most influential modernist architects and author of this construction built in 1962. The home is conceived as an open space expressed freely of conventions, without a doubt a feature of Neutra's work. His use of glass, as well as facilitating communication with the environment and a fluid interior, lends his structures an ethereal ambience and allowed him to manipulate natural light so that it penetrates every corner. Neutra knew how to bring together elements of science, technology and industrialisation without diminishing his sense of good taste.

Die Beziehung zwischen Mensch und Natur ist eine Konstante im Werk von Richard Neutra, einem der einflussreichsten modernen Architekten, der dieses Haus im Jahr 1962 erbaut hat. Das Haus ist als ein offener und innovativer Raum angelegt, ein Ausdruck der künstlerischen Freiheit der Arbeiten Neutras. Durch die Benutzung von Glas wird eine freie Kommunikation zwischen der Umgebung und dem Inneren geschaffen. Es entstanden ätherische Strukturen und Tageslicht fällt in alle Winkel ein. Neutra machte sich die Möglichkeiten der Wissenschaft, Technik und Industrialisierung zunutze, um mit deren Hilfe durchaus geschmackvolle Häuser zu gestalten.

Hees Neutra House

Architect: **Richard Neutra** Photos: © **Clare Beresford**

115

La relation entre l'homme et la nature est constante dans le travail de Richard Neutra, l'un des architectes modernes les plus influents et auteur de cette construction datant de 1962. Cette demeure est un espace ouvert, innovateur, libéré de toute convention, ce qui caractérise le travail de Neutra. L'usage du verre permet un communication libre et fluide avec l'environnement et crée des structures éthérées en manipulant à volonté la lumière qui pénètre de partout. Neutra sût conjuger avec habileté les possibilités que la science, la technologie et l'industrialisation lui offrirent sans pour autant diminuer son sens du bon goût.

La relación entre hombre y naturaleza es una constante en la obra de Richard Neutra, uno de los arquitectos modernos más influyentes y autor de esta construcción levantada en 1962. La vivienda se resuelve como un espacio abierto e innovador que expresa la libertad de convenciones que sin duda presidía el trabajo de Neutra. El uso del cristal le permite que la comunicación entre el entorno y los interiores fluya libremente, le ofrece la posibilidad de crear estructuras de trazos etéreos y le facilita el moldear la luz a voluntad para que ésta penetre por todos los rincones. Neutra supo conjugar con acierto las posibilidades que la ciencia, la técnica y la industrialización le ofrecían sin que por ello mermara en sus composiciones el buen gusto.

The basic principals of this home, that adapts and uses its setting to its maximum potential, are discretion and simplicity. The construction is flanked by thick vegetation, which isolates it from its neighbours. The contrast of its geometric, well-defined lines and the natural surrounding balance the overall project and produce an attractive interplay of tones and textures. The architectural strategies employed, such as substituting various walls for huge windows and the absence of doors, ensure that the communication between its functional and restrained interior and lush exterior is fluid and unbroken.

Das grundlegende Prinzip dieses Hauses, das sich perfekt an die Umgebung anpasst, ist Diskretion und Einfachheit. Der Bau ist von üppiger Vegetation umgeben, die ihn von den Nachbarhäusern abschirmt. Dieser Kontrast zwischen den geometrischen und klar definierten, architektonischen Linien und der Natur schafft ein Gleichgewicht und lässt ein interessantes Spiel von Tönen und Texturen entstehen. Durch die angewandten architektonischen Lösungen, die großen Fenster, die einige der Wände ersetzen und das Wegfallen von Türen, wurde eine konstante, fließende Kommunikation zwischen außen und den nüchternen, funktionellen Innenräumen geschaffen.

Bach House

Photos: © Ricardo Labougle

123

Les principes de base de cette maison, qui s'adapte à son environnement et l'exploite au maximum, sont la discrétion et la simplicité. La construction est entourée d'une végétation dense qui la cache et l'isole du voisinage. Ce contraste entre des lignes architecturales géométriques définies et l'environnement naturel, équilibre l'ensemble et crée un jeu de tonalités et de textures attrayant. Les solutions architecturales employées, tels que la substitution de certaines parois par de grandes baies vitrées, ou l'absence de portes, assurent une communication fluide et constante entre un intérieur sobre et fonctionnel et un extérieur luxuriant.

El principio básico de esta vivienda, que se adapta al entorno y sabe sacarle el máximo partido, es la discreción y la sencillez. La construcción se encuentra rodeada de una de una frondosa vegetación que la oculta y la aísla de sus vecinos. Ese contraste entre unas líneas arquitectónicas geométricas y bien definidas y el entorno natural equilibra el conjunto y dibuja un atractivo juego de tonalidades y texturas. Las soluciones arquitectónicas empleadas, como la sustitución de algunas paredes por grandes ventanales o la eliminación de puertas, consiguen que la comunicación entre los interiores –sobrios y funcionales– y el exterior sea constante y fluida.

This 170 m² loft is part of a building that was originally constructed in 1919. The layout permits an uninterrupted visual flow and evocative and efficient spatial continuity in which the pieces of furniture define and mark the boundaries of the different living areas. The designer and artist Dorian la Padura was put in charge of the interior decoration: modern and functional interiors in which a skilful and thought-provoking mixture of styles, colours and forms are placed together. The result is a dynamic space with a grand chromatic richness; a homage to diversity and eclecticism.

Das Originalgebäude, in dem sich dieses ungefähr 170 m² große Loft befindet, wurde 1919 erbaut. Das Loft ist so angelegt, dass man einen freien Blick hat und der Raum nicht unterbrochen wird. Die Möbel und die Dekorationselemente definieren und begrenzen die einzelnen Bereiche. Dorian La Padura hat hier mit großer Treffsicherheit avantgardistische und funktionelle Räume gestaltet, in denen verschiedene Stile, Trends und Formen aufeinander treffen. Das Ergebnis ist ein dynamischer, farbenfroher und reicher Raum. Eine Hommage an die Mischung und den Eklektizismus.

Dorian Loft

135

Interior Designer: **Dorian La Padura**   Photos: © **Clare Beresford**

Cet appartement de 170 m² est dans un bâtiment qui fût construit en 1919. Les différents niveaux de ce projet offrent un liberté visuelle et une continuité de l'espace, dans laquelle les meubles et les éléments de décoration ont pour but de définir et de délimiter chaque domaine. Le dessinateur et artiste Dorian la Padura fût chargé de concevoir avec habileté un intérieur moderne, avant-gardiste et fonctionel où cohabitent de façon suggestive divers styles, tendances et formes. Il en résulte un espace dynamique et riche en couleurs. Un hommage à la diversité et à l'éclectisme.

El edificio original que acoge este loft de unos 170 m² fue construido en 1919. El proyecto traza una distribución en planta que permite la liberación visual y una sugerente y eficaz continuidad espacial en que las piezas de mobiliario y los elementos decorativos se encargan de definir y delimitar cada una de las áreas. El diseñador y artista Dorian La Padura se ha encargado de resolver, con gran habilidad, unos interiores vanguardistas y funcionales en los que conviven una sugerente diversidad de estilos, tendencias y formas. El resultado es un espacio dinámico, de gran cromatismo y riqueza. Todo un homenaje al mestizaje y al eclecticismo.

137

Two contained geometric volumes joined at their longest side define the pre-existing structure of this nineteen-fifties home. Its renovation and extension managed to achieve a
creation of generous volumes that hold two parallelepiped rectangular bodies united by
an extensive galvanised metal roof. The wall that surrounds the pool extends to the
new concrete parameter finished in blue stucco that defines the garden area, pulls in
the garage and the main door and penetrates the interior of the home's reception and
living area.

Das aus den fünfziger Jahren stammende Gebäude bestand aus zwei geometrischen Con-
tainern, die auf der Längsseite miteinander verbunden waren. Durch die Erweiterung und
den Umbau ist ein Gebäude mit großzügigen Formen entstanden, das die beiden fla-
chen, parallelen und rechteckigen Formen beibehalten hat und sie durch ein großes
Dach aus galvanisierten Metalllamellen vereint. Die Mauer um den Swimmingpool wurde bis zu der neuen, blau verputzten Betonwand verlängert, die den Garten begrenzt, die
Garage mit dem Haupteingang verbindet und bis ins Innere dringt, indem sie durch die
Galerie geführt wird, die den Zugang zu den Wohnräumen bildet.

Arango-berry House

Architect: **Franklin D. Israel** Photos: © **Richard Bryant/Arcaid**

139

Ce bâtiment datant des années cinquante, était composé de deux containers liés entre
eux sur leur longueur. En l'agrandissant et le transformant, on a obtenu un bâtiment
aux formes généreuses ayant gardé ses formes parallèles, rectangulaires et planes,
qui ont été réunies par un toit galvanisé formé de lamelles métaliques. Le mur entou-
rant la piscine fût prolongé jusqu'à la nouvelle paroi de béton, crépie en bleu. Cette paroi délimite le jardin, relie le garage à l'entrée principale et se poursuit jusqu'à l'intérieur en conduisant à travers la galerie qui constitue l'accès à l'habitation.

Dos contenedores geométricos unidos definían el volumen preexistente de esta vivienda,
cuya estructura original fue construida en los años 50. El resultado de la ampliación
ha logrado dibujar un conjunto de dimensiones generosas manteniendo los dos cuerpos paralelepípedos rectangulares unificados por una cubierta revestida en lámina me-
tálica galvanizada. El muro que circunda la piscina se alargó hasta el nuevo paramen-
to de hormigón estucado en azul que se encarga de limitar el jardín, relacionar el nuevo
garaje con la puerta principal y penetrar hasta el interior de la vivienda al franquear la
galería de acceso a la zona de estar.

The alterations of this apartment situated in downtown L.A. follows the basic rules of modern architecture. The exact organisation of space allows the interior (conceived as a series of open, continuous spaces) to be perfectly defined and the careful selec-tion of materials fill the space with a peaceful, modern and timeless ambience. The insistence of combining pristine steel and glass with the warmth of wood creates a balanced living area, in which light is the fundamental element. From within the essence of this vital and captivating city is captured by the visual contact between exterior and interior.

Die Renovierung dieses Appartements in Downtown folgte den grundlegenden Regeln der zeitgenössischen Architektur. Die treffsichere Raumaufteilung schuf offene und fortlaufende Räume, die dennoch perfekt definiert sind. Durch eine sorgfältige Auswahl der Materialien entstand eine harmonische, avantgardistische und zeitlose Atmosphäre. Die kalte Textur von Stahl und Glas wurde mit der Wärme des Holzes kombiniert. So entstand ein ausgeglichenes Wohnambiente, in dem das Licht das wichtigste Element ist und das die Essenz dieser lebendigen und bezaubernden Stadt einfängt, da der Blickkontakt zwischen außen und innen stets aufrecht erhalten wird.

Noonan Apartment 143

Architect: **SPF:a (Stenfors Pali Fekete Architects)** Photos: © **John Linden**

La remise à neuf de cet appartement au centre ville suivit les règles fondamentales de l'architecture contemporaine. La justesse de l'aménagement offre des pièces ouvertes passant de l'une à l'autre et qui sont pour autant très définies. De par le choix soigneux des divers matériaux naît une atmosphère avant-gardiste et harmonieuse. La froideur de l'acier et du verre est combinée à la chaleur du bois. Cela crée une ambiance très agréable, dans laquelle la lumière joue un rôle essentiel, et qui réussit à capter l'essence de cette ville charmante et très vivante dû au contact visuel permanent avec l'extérieur.

La reforma de este apartamento situado en el Downtown sigue las reglas básicas de la arquitectura contemporánea. La organización espacial permite que los interiores –concebidos como espacios abiertos y continuos– queden definidos y la cuidada selección de materiales confiere al ambiente una atmósfera sosegada, vanguardista y atemporal. El empeño en aunar la fría textura del acero y el cristal con la calidez de la madera consigue dibujar una vivienda equilibrada en la que la luz es un elemento primordial y desde donde es posible capturar la esencia de una ciudad cautivadora al existir contacto visual entre interior y exterior.

Facing the sea on Hermosa Beach in the West of Los Angeles, the huge plates of glass connected to the exterior in the living areas act as the heart of this home which is distributed over a series of three vertical levels. If one of the facades is an enormous, closed volume of chipboard that spills over into the exterior, the other, is a transparent body open to the sea. This concept of opposed elements (open-closed, heavy-light) creates a stimulating inter-play of tensions. Against a cautious interior, the true appeal of this home is the architecture.

Am Sandstrand Hermosa Beach im Westen von L.A. liegt dieses Haus mit einem großen, verglasten Bau, in dem sich die Wohnräume mit unmittelbarem Kontakt nach außen befinden. Der verglaste Bereich ist das Zentrum des Hauses, das sich vertikal über drei Ebenen erstreckt. Eine der Fassaden ist geschlossen und massiv, während sich die andere, zum Strand gelegene, transparente Fassade, zum Meer öffnet. Diese Anwendung verschiedener Konzepte (offen-geschlossen, massiv-leicht...) schafft ein anziehendes Spiel der Spannungen. Die Architektur ist der eigentliche Hauptdarsteller, was durch die zurückhaltende Dekoration noch unterstrichen wird.

Reyna Residence

Architect: **Dean Nota Architect, AIA** Interior design: **Marina Mizruh**

Photos: © **Erhard Pfeiffer**

149

Cette maison, se trouve sur la plage de Hermosa Beach, à l'ouest de L.A. Cet édifice de verre permet aux différentes pièces d'avoir un contact direct avec l'extérieur. L'espace vitré est le centre de cette construction qui est érigée à la verticale sur trois niveaux. L'une des facades est massive et fermée, tandis que l'autre, côté plage est transparente et s'ouvre sur la mer. L'application de ces différents conceptes (ouvert-fermé, massif-léger) crée un jeux de tensions très intéressant. L'architecture en est l'acteur principal, ce qui vient encore accentué par une décoration très réservée.

Emplazado frente al mar, en contacto con la arena de la playa Hermosa Beach, al oeste de Los Ángeles: un gran volumen acristalado que contiene las áreas de estar y se comunica con el exterior se convierte en el corazón de esta vivienda organizada en una secuencia vertical de tres niveles. Si una de las fachadas es un volumen cerrado y macizo que se vuelca al exterior, la otra, que da a la playa, es un cuerpo transparente abierto al mar. Ese empleo de conceptos encontrados (abierto-cerrado, solidez-ligereza...) se encarga de crear un sugerente juego de tensiones. La arquitectura es la verdadera protagonista potenciada por una decoración mesurada.

Section

Elevations

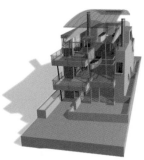
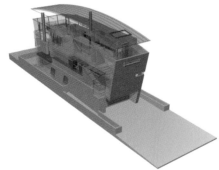

Axonometric perspectives

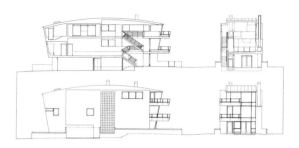

Section

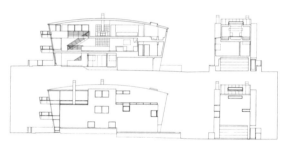

Section

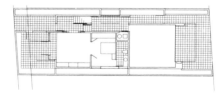

Ground floor

This home is a good representation of quintessential L.A. style in which existing, unordered forms and new volumes are precisely adjusted so as not to cause further chaos. Lehrer Architects, the studio in charge of re-modelling the home, was confronted with a series of obstacles. On one hand, the old ranch-style homestead had been personalised over the years with various extensions and alterations and on the other the renovations had to maintain the spirit of the original construction whilst converting it into a contemporary abode. The result is a home charged with personality in which the past and present live together harmoniously.

Dieses Haus ist die Quintessenz des Designs in L.A. In anderen Worten: chaotische Formen werden an neue Bauten angepasst, ohne dass das architektonische Chaos größer wird. Lehrer Architects, die die Renovierung und Erweiterung des Hauses durchführten, stießen auf eine Reihe von Bedingungen, die Grenzen setzten. Es handelt sich um eine ehemalige Ranch im eklektischen Stil mit Anbauten späteren Datums; und die neuen Formen mussten sich dem Originalgebäude anpassen, aber gleichzeitig sollte das Gebäude modern werden. Das Ergebnis ist ein Wohngebäude mit betontem Eigencharakter, in dem eine Harmonie zwischen Vergangenheit und Gegenwart erreicht wurde.

Belson Residence

161

Architect: **Lehrer Architects** Photos: © **Michael B. Leher AIA & Grant Mudford**

Cette maison représente la quintessence du design à L.A. En d'autres mots, des formes chaotiques viennent adaptées à des constructions nouvelles, sans que le chaos architectural n'empire. Lehrers Architects furent chargés de rénover et d'agrandir cette maison. Ils furent confrontés à des conditions qui leur imposèrent certaines limites. Il s'agissait d'un ranch de style eclectique, auquel on avait rajouté diverses annexes au fil des années. Les formes nouvelles devant être adaptées au bâtiment d'origine, tout en le modernisant. Le résultat est une construction au caractère prononcé, où le passé et le présent sont en harmonie.

Esta casa representa la quintaesencia del diseño en Los Ángeles, que es conseguir ajustar unas formas caóticas a unos nuevos volúmenes sin potenciar el caos arquitectónico. Los responsables de proyectar la nueva reforma y ampliación de la vivienda, Lehrer Architects, se encontraron con una serie de condicionantes que no podían obviar. Por un lado se trataba de un antiguo rancho de estilo ecléctico al que ya se le habían añadadido algunos cuerpos a lo largo de los años y, por otro, las nuevas formas debían permitir mantener el espíritu de la construcción original a la vez que se conseguía una edificación actual. El resultado ha sido una vivienda cargada de personalidad en la que conviven sin alterarse presente y pasado.

162

The home hovers between the majesty of the past and contemporary structural innovations. A suggestive elegance runs through the interior of the building that seamlessly brings together the past and present whilst taking full advantage of both. The visual and stylistic richness of its interior is only comparable to its spectacular views that can be seem from every angle of its surroundings. Daring blends of colour, a suggestive fusion of styles and tendencies that show how intelligent blending can enrich and even provide practical and efficient solutions; an architectural 'mise en scene' that is a triumph of imagination.

Dieses Haus bewegt sich zwischen der Pracht der Vergangenheit und moderneren, konstruktiven Lösungen. In den eleganten Räumen dieses Gebäudes sind die Vergangenheit und Gegenwart problemlos und perfekt miteinander kombiniert. Der visuelle und stilistische Reichtum der Räume kann nur mit dem überwältigenden Ausblick, den man auf die Umgebung hat, verglichen werden. Gewagte Farbspiele und eine interessante Mischung von Stilen und Trends beweisen, dass die perfekte Vermischung bereichert und praktische, effiziente Lösungen bietet. Vermischung und Fantasie in großzügiger Inszenierung.

Codiko House

Architect: **Kevin Cozen** Photos: © **Clare Beresford**

165

Cette habitation navigue entre la majesté du passé et les modes de construction actuels. Une élégance certaine parcourt l'intérieur de cette maison qui associe sans perturbation le passé au présent en tirant le meilleur parti des deux. La richesse visuelle et stylistique de son intérieur n'est comparable qu'à la vue panoramique spectaculaire que l'on a des alentours. Un jeu de couleurs osé, un amalgame suggestif de styles et de tendances qui démontre qu'un mélange intelligent peut enrichir et même apporter des solutions pratiques et éficaces et une mise en scène généreuse rendent hommage à l'imagination.

Esta vivienda navega entre la majestuosidad del pasado y las soluciones constructivas más actuales. Una sugerente elegancia recorre los interiores de esta edificación que conjuga sin traumas pasado y presente sabiendo sacar el máximo partido de ambos. La riqueza visual y estilística de sus interiores sólo es comparable a la espectacularidad de las vistas panorámicas que pueden contemplarse del entorno. Atrevidos juegos cromáticos, una sugerente amalgama de estilos y tendencias que demuestran que las mezclas bien resueltas enriquecen y aportan soluciones tan prácticas como eficaces y una generosa puesta en escena rinden tributo al mestizaje y a la imaginación.

Despite the theatrics of its appearance, there is nothing gratuitous or arbitrary in this imposing and peculiar home. Carried out in the architectural language of Eric Owen Moss, he remained faithful to some very stringent ideas that reflect his obsession for details and integral design. This experiment in form and space converts the kitchen into the nerve centre of the home. Its unusual conical forms become the main exterior volume, delimiting other structural forms, and are also the principal element from which the interior space is laid-out.

Beeindruckend und eigenartig. Obwohl das Gebäude sehr theatralisch aussieht, wurde hier nichts dem Zufall überlassen. Die formelle Sprache, die der Architekt Eric Owen Moss anwendet, folgt sehr konkreten Ideen, welche seine Bemühungen um das Detail und die einheitliche Gestaltung zeigen. Das Experiment mit der Form und dem Raum macht aus der Küche das Rückgrat des Hauses. Ihre einzigartigen Kegelformen machen sie von außen zum Hauptteil des Gebäudes, und dieser Körper begrenzt und erzeugt die übrigen Strukturformen. Auch die Raumaufteilung im Inneren geht von der Küche aus.

Lawson Western House

Architect: **Eric Owen Moss** Photos: © **Tom Bonner**

Impressionnant et étrange. Bien que ce bâtiment ait un aspect très théatral, rien n'est dû au hasard. Le langage formel employé par l'architecte Eric Owen Moss, suit des idées très concrètes qui montrent la peine qu'il met dans les détails et dans l'uniformité de la réalisation. L'expérimentation avec la forme et l'espace font de la cuisine, la partie la plus importante de la maison. Sa forme conique très particulière en font, vu du dehors, le point principal de la construction. Cet élément délimite et fait naître à la fois les autres forme de la structure. La répartition des autres pièces part également de la cuisine.

Imponente y peculiar. A pesar de la teatralidad de su apariencia, en esta vivienda nada es gratuito o arbitrario: el lenguaje formal empleado por el arquitecto Eric Owen Moss obedece a la aplicación de unas ideas muy concretas que reflejan su preocupación por los detalles y el diseño integral. La experimentación –tanto formal como espacial– convierte a la cocina en el eje vertebrador de la casa; sus singulares formas cónicas la convierten en el volumen principal en el exterior –este cuerpo delimita y genera el resto de formas estructurales– y en el elemento a partir del cual se organiza el espacio interior.

Ground floor

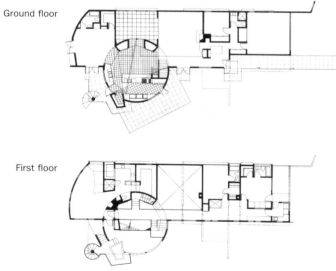

First floor

Some rational, concise and defined geometric lines mark this construction. Its hermetic and frail exterior presence is soon forgotten upon entering the interior of the home. The concise spatial layout manages to configure a series of transparent and open interior spaces that communicate with the exterior through its multiple glass openings of various sizes. Restricted measurements and a decorative austerity are the star features of this modern home where nothing is superfluous. Here nothing has been left to chance and every element has its purpose.

Dieser Bau wird von rationellen, präzisen und definierten geometrischen Linien geprägt. Wenn man das Gebäude von außen betrachtet, wirkt die Architektur hermetisch und kalt, wenn man jedoch das Innere betritt, entsteht ein vollständig anderer Eindruck. Durch die gelungene Raumaufteilung entstanden transparente und offene Räume, die durch zahlreiche, verglaste Öffnungen in verschiedenen Größen eine Verbindung nach außen herstellen. Der sparsame Einsatz der Mittel und die nüchterne Dekoration kennzeichnen diese moderne Wohnung, in der es keine überflüssigen Elemente gibt. Nichts befindet sich zufällig irgendwo, für alles gibt es einen Grund.

Kohli Residence

Architect: **Frank Glynn** Photos: © **Michael Herbach**

179

Ce bâtiment est empreint de lignes géométriques définies, précises et rationelles. Considéré de l'extérieur, son architecture paraît hermétique et froide, mais lorsqu'on y pénètre on a une impression totalement différente. La répartition des pièces est très réussie. Il en résulte un espace ouvert et transparent, qui est soutenu par de nombreuses ouvertures vitrées de tailles différentes établissant un contact avec l'extérieur. L'emploi parcimonieux de moyens et une décoration sobre, distinguent ce logement moderne, dans lequel on ne rencontre aucun élément superflu. Rien ne se trouve là par hasard il y a une raison à tout.

Unas racionales, concisas y definidas líneas geométricas marcan a esta construcción. Su presencia exterior podría inducir a errores ya que el hermetismo y frialdad que su arquitectura transmite quedan totalmente eliminados al penetrar en el interior de la vivienda. La acertada organización espacial logra configurar unos interiores diáfanos y abiertos que se comunican con el exterior gracias a múltiples aberturas acristaladas de tamaños diferentes. Economía de medios y austeridad decorativa son los protagonistas de esta residencia contemporánea en la que no existen elementos superfluos. Nada está allí por azar, todo tiene una razón de ser.

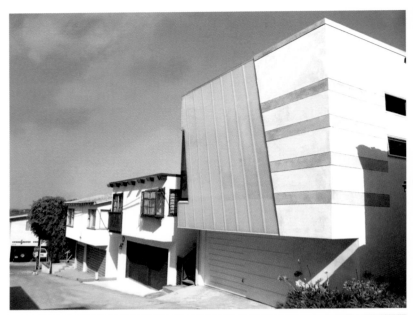

Plans

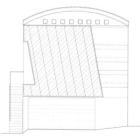

Elevation

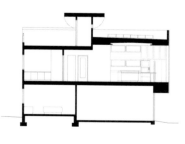

Section

Originally constructed in the mid-sixties, the owner of this home (situated on a hill over-
looking the city) decided to remodel the existing building and add an annexe with the
purpose of capturing Southern California's sense of light and space. A wish that takes
shape in its highly illuminated open spaces in which exterior and interior melt into one
and where a refined and emotive palette of materials, textures and colours dominate.
The rigorous selection of furniture —all modern design classics— highlight the work's
gloriously rational architectural style.

Ursprünglich wurde dieses Gebäude, das auf einer Anhöhe über die Stadt ragt, Mitte der
sechziger Jahre erbaut. Der Eigentümer begann mit dem Umbau des existierenden Hauses und fügte ihm einen Anbau zu, mit dem die besondere Essenz des Lichtes und des
Raums im Süden Kaliforniens eingefangen werden sollte. Dieser Wunsch materialisier-
te sich in hellen und offenen Räumen, in denen sich die Grenzen zwischen innen und
außen verwischen und die von edlen und ansprechenden Materialien, Texturen und Farben dominiert werden. Die sorgfältige Auswahl der Möbel, wahre Klassiker des zeitgenössischen Designs, unterstreicht noch die rationalistische und erlesene Architektur.

Laccone Residence

Architect: **Marmol-Radziner + Associates**   Photos: © **Ricardo Labougle**

185

Cet immeuble fût construit dans les années 60, sur une coline qui surplombe la ville. Les
propriétaires transformèrent la partie existante et l'agrandirent, en essayant de capter
la luminosité de la Califonie du sud. Ce désir se trouva matérialisé par des pièces claires et ouvertes desquelles les frontières entre l'intérieur et l'extérieur s'estompent.
Matériaux nobles, textures et couleurs dominent. La sélection soigneuse des meubles,
des classiques du design contemporain, soulignent encore la rationalité de cette architecture de choix.

Construida originalmente a mediados de los 60, el propietario de esta vivienda –situada
en una colina desde la que se domina la ciudad– decidió remodelar la edificación existente y añadir un anexo con la intención de captar la particular esencia de la luz y el
espacio del sur de California. Un deseo que se materializa en espacios luminosos y
abiertos, en los que las fronteras entre interior y exterior se confunden y en los que
reina una refinada y sugerente paleta de materiales, texturas y colores. La cuidada selección de piezas de mobiliario –auténticos clásicos del diseño contemporáneo– se encarga de potenciar una arquitectura racionalista y exquisita.

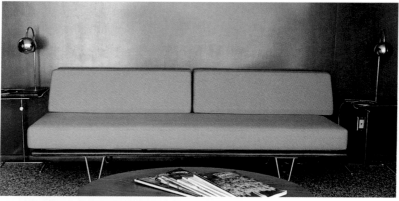

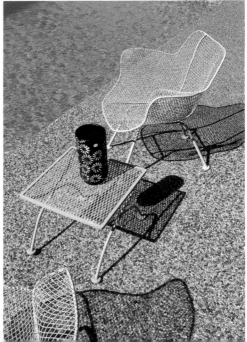

When confronted with the challenge of remodelling this home, the architects conceived the project from the original structure, designed in 1963 by Conrad Buff, Calvin Straub and Don Hensman. As well as reforming the original dwelling, the intervention allowed an extension that serves as a studio-office. This symmetric floor strengthens the dialogue between the interior and exterior. The conjunction of the building's original lines and the new avant-guard architectural solutions were given the utmost attention at every moment, and, in the end, emphasised the simplicity of an already exceptional structure.

Die Architekten planten den Umbau dieses Hauses basierend auf der bereits 1963 von Conrad Buff, Calvin Straub und Don Hensman erbauten Struktur. Das Haus wurde nicht nur renoviert, sondern es wurde auch ein Anbau hinzugefügt, der als Atelier und Büro genutzt wird. Es handelt sich um einen Bau mit symmetrischem Grundriss, der den Dialog zwischen innen und außen potenziert. Auch dem Zusammenspiel zwischen den originalen Linien und den avantgardistischen und moderneren Lösungen wurde große Aufmerksamkeit geschenkt, um so die Einfachheit des bereits vorhandenen, wundervollen Gebäudes zu unterstreichen.

Katleman Residence

Architect: **Marmol-Radziner + Associates** Photos: © **Benny Chan**

197

Confrontés aux travaux de transformation de cette maison, les architectes conçurent ce projet à partir de la structure existante, dessinée en 1963 par Conrad Buff, Calvin Straub et Don Hensman. En plus de la réformation de la construction, on pût y ajouter une annexe servant de zone bureau/studio. Il s'agit d'une construction de surfaces symétriques renforçant le dialogue entre l'intérieur et l'extérieur. On a prêté grande attention à la conjonction entre les lignes d'origine et les solutions plus actuelles et avant-gardistes afin d'augmenter la simplicité d'un espace déjà plus que privilégié.

Al enfrentarse a las obras de remodelación de esta vivienda, los arquitectos concibieron el proyecto a partir de la estructura existente diseñada en 1963 por Conrad Buff, Calvin Straub y Don Hensman. La intervención, además de reformar la construcción, permitió añadir un volumen anexo que funciona como zona de estudio-despacho. Se trata de una edificación de planta simétrica en la que se ha potenciado el diálogo entre interior y exterior y se ha prestado atención a que la conjunción entre las líneas originales y las soluciones más vanguardistas y actuales fueran de la mano en todo momento y enfatizaran la simplicidad de un espacio ya de por sí privilegiado.

Spectacular architecture and heady panoramic views define this home of unbroken, white, geometric volumes. Simplicity stands out in the interior where the tonality of pale, white walls is only occasionally interrupted by the colourful touches in furniture and furnishings. These only serve to emphasise the extreme light and generous dimensions of a highly contemporary, minimalist and elegant home. The exterior's star feature is a pool whose inviting depth is hard to resist.

Die beeindruckende Architektur und schwindelerregenden Aussichten definieren dieses Wohnhaus aus gleichmäßigen, weißen, geometrischen Formen. Die Räume zeichnen sich durch ihre Einfachheit aus, die Weiße der Wände, öfters durch die Farbtupfer der Möbel und Dekorationselemente unterbrochen, fällt ins Auge und verstärkt die Helligkeit und die großzügigen Dimensionen des Raums, der modern, minimalistisch und elegant gestaltet ist. Das wichtigste Element im Freien ist der Swimmingpool, von dem aus man den Abgrund betrachten kann, den man zu seinen Füßen ahnt.

Maurice House

209

Architect: **Brent Saville** Photos: © **Peter Polster**

Une architecture spectaculaire et un panorama vertigineux définissent cette maison constituée de volumes géométriques blancs et solides. Une grande simplicité se dégage de cet intérieur dans lequel la pâleur des parois ne vient interrompue qu'occasionnellement par les touches colorées des meubles et des éléments de décoration. Ceux-ci ne servant qu'à augmenter la luminosité et les dimensions généreuses de cette demeure contemporaine, minimaliste et pourtant élégante. A l'extérieur, la piscine est l'acteur principal qui invite à contempler les profondeurs s'ouvrant à nos pieds.

Una arquitectura espectacular y unas panorámicas de vértigo definen esta vivienda de consistentes y blancos volúmenes geométricos. La simplicidad recorre unos interiores en los que llama poderosamente la atención la blanca palidez de sus paredes –tonalidad que se rompe en contadas ocasiones con los toques cromáticos del mobiliario y los elementos decorativos–, que no hace más que potenciar una luminosidad extrema y las generosas dimensiones del espacio impregnado de un estilo actual, minimalista y elegante. Por su parte, en el exterior una piscina que invita a contemplar el abismo que se intuye a sus pies se convierte en la protagonista.

213

The project for the extension of this home was founded on a maximum respect for the qualities of the original structure and that the pre-existing volumes were not annulled when the new ones were added. It needed to transform one of the ranch's wings and also create new living areas. The communication between exterior and interior is constant upon opening the rear façade to the garden. The sea view is uninterrupted, as is the immediate countryside that can be enjoyed in a fluid and constant manner. The result creates an endearing play on light and shade and between what is visible and what is merely suggested.

Bei der Planung der Erweiterung dieses Wohnhauses wurde das Originalgebäude so weit wie möglich respektiert, und die bereits vorhandenen Gebäudeteile wurden durch die neuen Anbauten nicht annulliert. Durch den Eingriff musste einer der Flügel der Ranch umgebaut werden, um neue Räume zu schaffen. Die hintere Fassade öffnet sich zum Garten und stellt so eine konstante Verbindung zwischen innen und außen her. Man hat einen ununterbrochenen Blick auf den Ozean und auf die innere Landschaft, die fließend und konstant wirkt. Ein attraktives Spiel mit Licht und Schatten, zwischen dem, was man sieht, und dem, was man ahnt.

Ziering Residence

Architect: **Paul Murdoch** Photos: © **Grant Mudford**

En planifiant l'agrandissement de cette maison, on essaya de respecter autant que possible le bâtiment d'origine. Les parties existantes ne furent pas remplacés par les élément nouveaux. Cette opération nécessitai la transformation d'une des ailes du ranch, afin de créer des pièces supplémentaires. La façade antérieure s'ouvre sur le jardin, établissant une liaison continue entre le dehors et le dedans. On a un coup d'oeil sur l'océan et le paysage, qui glisse et se fond quasiment, paraissant ininterrompu. Un jeu d'ombre et de lumière très attrayant entre ce que l'on voit et ce que l'on devine.

Al proyectar la ampliación de esta vivienda se buscaba respetar al máximo las cualidades de la edificación original y lograr que los volúmenes preexistentes no quedaran anulados al añadir los nuevos elementos constructivos. La intervención debía transformar una de las alas del rancho y permitir crear nuevas estancias. La comunicación entre interior y exterior es constante al abrir las fachadas traseras al jardín. La visión del océano es ininterrumpida, así como la del paisaje interior, que puede observarse de manera constante y fluida. Un atractivo juego entre luces y sombras, entre lo que queda a la vista y lo que se intuye.

First floor

Ground floor

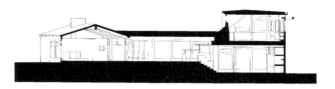

Sections

Situated in the hills of Santa Monica, the volumes of this home (whose original construction dates back to 1930) are integrated into its surroundings, accentuating the particular topographic characteristics of the landscape. The architectural approach employed here has managed to create a suggestive play on contrasts between horizontal and vertical lines to achieve a harmonious and almost rhythmical composition. The interior of the home, organised on different levels that open out onto the exterior, moves between stylistic richness, diversity, calm and tranquillity.

Der ursprüngliche Bau dieses in den Bergen von Santa Monica gelegenen Wohnhauses stammt aus dem Jahr 1930. Seine Formen passen sich an die Umgebung an und akzentuieren die typischen topographischen Formen der Region. Die verwendeten, architektonischen Lösungen lassen ein anregendes Spiel mit Gegensätzen entstehen, zwischen horizontalen und vertikalen Linien, aus denen sich eine harmonische Komposition und eine rhythmische Präsenz ergibt. Die stilistisch sehr vielfältigen, abwechslungsreichen, aber dennoch ruhig wirkenden Räume des Hauses sind auf verschiedenen Ebenen angelegt und haben an der Landschaft teil, indem sie sich nach außen öffnen.

Gainsborough House

Architect: **Sant Architects**   Photos: © **Marvin Rand**

Cette maison qui se trouve dans les montagnes de Santa Monica, fût construite en 1930. Ses formes sont adaptées à son environnement et accentue la topographie typique de cette région. Les solutions architecturales choisies permettent de jouer avec des contrastes intéressants, entre les lignes horizontales et verticales. Il en ressort une composition harmonieuse et une présence très rythmée. Les pièces ont un style très varié et changeant d'où se répend pourtant la tranquilité. Elles sont réparties sur différents niveaux et font partie du paysage, du fait qu'elles donnent et s'ouvrent sur l'extérieur.

Situada en las montañas de Santa Mónica, los volúmenes de esta vivienda –cuyos contornos originales son de 1930– se integran en el entorno acentuando las particulares características topográficas que definen el enclave. Las soluciones arquitectónicas empleadas consiguen dibujar un sugerente juego de contrastes entre líneas horizontales y verticales que le conceden a la composición una armónica y rítmica presencia. Los interiores de la vivienda, organizados en diferentes niveles y que participan también del paisaje al abrirse al exterior, se mueven entre la riqueza estilística, la diversidad, la calma y la tranquilidad.

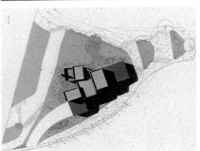

Location plan

Floor plans

Sections

Section

Section

Surrounded by nature and dominated by some splendid vistas, this recently re-modelled home was constructed in 1955. The work carried out has managed to maintain the home's original essence and at the same time adapt to new necessities. Sobriety and a precise organisation of space dominate, as do the discreet and well-blended use of materials, colours and textures featured in the different living areas. The result is a series of warm and welcoming interiors reigned by functionality, elegance and restraint.

Dieses vor kurzem renovierte Haus aus dem Jahr 1955 befindet sich inmitten der Natur und man genießt einen beeindruckenden Ausblick. Trotz dieses Eingriffs wurde die ursprüngliche Essenz des Hauses beibehalten, und gleichzeitig wurden die Räume an die heutigen Ansprüche angepasst. Nüchternheit und eine perfekte Organisation des Raumes bestimmen das Haus, ebenso die diskrete und gut aufeinander abgestimmte Palette an Materialien, Farben und Texturen, welche die Räume effizient unterteilen. Das Ergebnis sind warme, einladende und natürliche Räume, in denen Funktionalität, Eleganz und Zurückhaltung dominieren.

Elle House

233

Architect: **Zoran Wyndrich** Photos: © **Peter Polster**

Cette maison qui a été rénovée récemment fût construite en 1955. Elle est encrée en pleine nature et jouit d'une vue splendide. On a essayer de garder le caractère d'origine tout en l'adaptant aux nécessités actuelles. La sobriété et une répartition très réussie des pièces dominent, ainsi qu'un mélange discrêt de divers matériaux, textures et couleurs qui définissent les différents espaces. Le résultat est un intérieur chaleureux, accueillant, exempt de tout artifice qui se distingue par sa fonctionnalité, son élégance et sa contenance.

Anclada en medio de la naturaleza y dominada por unas espléndidas vistas, esta vivienda, recientemente remodelada, fue construida en 1955. La intervención ha conseguido mantener la esencia original a la vez que ha adaptado el espacio a las necesidades actuales. La sobriedad y la acertada organización espacial son la tónica dominante, al igual que una conjugada y discreta paleta de materiales, colores y texturas que resuelven con eficacia las diferentes estancias. El resultado son unos interiores cálidos, acogedores y exentos de artificios que se rigen por los principios de la funcionalidad, la elegancia y la contención.

The renovation of this home had to accommodate some precise requirements set down by the owner: create a modern dwelling without discounting the original 1930 building. The final result is a structure where new volumes have been added that respect the home's original identity and where past and present reside together effortlessly. The natural Californian light that bathes the location invites relaxed contemplation of its natural beauty and panoramic vistas. A generous, serene and illuminated home laid out on two levels in which its glass walls offer a continuous view of the exterior.

Die Eigentümer hatten eine klare Vorstellung von der Renovierung ihres Hauses. Es sollte ein neues, modernes Haus entstehen, dessen Originalstruktur aus dem Jahr 1930 erhalten bleiben sollte. Das Endergebnis ist ein Gebäude mit Anbauten, welche die einzigartige, bereits vorhandene Struktur berücksichtigen und Vergangenheit und Gegenwart harmonisch vereinigen. Ein von dem einzigartigen Licht Kaliforniens gebadeter Ort, der zum Betrachten der umliegenden Natur und des wundervollen Ausblicks einlädt. Ein großzügiger, heller und ruhiger Raum organisiert das Wohnhaus, das auf zwei Ebenen liegt. Durch gläserne Wände blickt man stets nach draußen.

Kimura House

241

Architect: **Sant Architects** Photos: © **John Edward Linden**

Les propriétaires avaient une idée très précise pour la rénovation de leur maison. Ils désiraient obtenir un bâtiment moderne ayant gardé la structure originale des années 30. Le résultat est une construction ayant plusieures annexes qui tiennent compte de la structure existante et combinent harmonieusement le passé au présent. C'est un endroit inondé de cette luminosité particulière à la Californie qui invite à contempler la nature des alentours. Une grande pièce claire et tranquile est le noyau de cette maison qui est construite sur deux niveaux. Des grandes baies vitrées permettent d'avoir un contact constant avec l'extérieur.

Al abordar la intervención de reforma, los requerimientos del propietario fueron concisos: disponer de una nueva y moderna casa sin prescindir de la estructura original construida en 1930. El resultado final es una edificación a la que se han añadido volúmenes respetando la identidad singular existente y en donde pasado y presente conviven sin traumas. Un lugar bañado por la singular luz californiana que invita a la contemplación de la naturaleza que la envuelve y a disfrutar de las espectaculares vistas de las que dispone. Un generoso espacio luminoso y sereno organiza la vivienda, distribuida en dos niveles. El empleo de paredes acristaladas posibilita una visión continua del exterior.

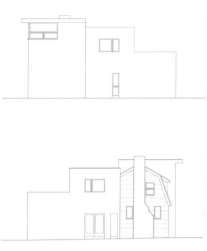

Elevations

Section

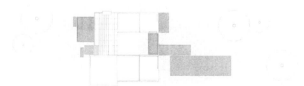

Location plan

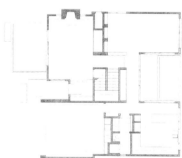

Ground floor

First floor

This location's topographical characteristics and the profession of the owner (painter) determined the volumes and layout of this home-studio. Taking into account the dimensions of the land, situated close to the sea on a rather small plot limited by two homes on its southern face and streets to the north, east and west, a vertical construction was decided upon. The final composition achieved an attractive interaction of flat surfaces and volumes that fit perfectly into place with the urban collage that surrounds it.

Die topographischen Besonderheiten, die Dimensionen des Ortes (nahe am Meer und auf einer nicht allzu großen, dreieckigen Parzelle gelegen, mit zwei Gebäuden im Süden und Straßen im Norden, Osten und Westen) und der Beruf des Eigentümers (Maler) bestimmten die architektonischen Konzepte und die Raumaufteilung dieses Wohnhauses und Ateliers. Aufgrund dieser Bedingungen wurde das Haus vertikal angelegt. So entstand ein attraktives Zusammenspiel von Ebenen, welche die Collage und urbanistische Vermischung der umgebenden Gebäude wiederspiegeln.

Marsh Residence

253

Architect: **Dean Nota Architect, AIA** Photos: © **Samuel Nugroho**

Dans la conception et l'agencement de cette maison, on a dû tenir compte de différents critères : Tout d'abord des particularités topographiques et des dimensions de l'endroit (située proche de la mer sur une parcelle rectangulaire n'étant pas très grande, avec deux bâtiments au sud et des routes au nord, à l'est et à l'ouest), ainsi que du mètier du propriétaire qui est peintre. Dans ces conditions cette maison fût construite à la verticale. Il en résulte un jeu attrayant des divers niveaux reflétant un mélange d'urbanisme et d'agglomération des bâtiments environnants.

Las particularidades topográficas, las dimensiones del lugar (localizada muy cerca del mar y situada en una parcela triangular no demasiado grande que limita con dos estructuras residenciales en su cara sur y se encuentra rodeada de calles a norte, este y oeste) y la profesión del propietario (pintor) determinaron los volúmenes arquitectónicos y la organización espacial de esta vivienda-estudio. Estos condicionantes han trazado una construcción que se desarrolla en vertical. La composición obtenida es una atractiva interacción de planos y volúmenes que representa ese collage y mestizaje urbanístico de los edificios que la rodean.

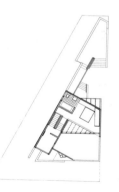

This residence's basic structure consists of three tectonic floors. Moving between the past, present and future, the architect Frank Fitzgibbons experimented with contrasts with great precision: open-closed, light-shade and heavy-light. This subtle inter-play of opposites appears as much in the exterior as the interior which is dominated in some areas by a cold, transparent atmosphere and in others by the warmth of wood with the occasional splash of colour. The interior spaces, decorated with exquisite austerity, are laid out according to their function with the communal areas on the lower floors and more private spaces in the upper area.

Drei Stockwerke strukturieren dieses Haus. Der Architekt Frank Fitzgibbons kombinierte meisterhaft Vergangenheit, Gegenwart und Zukunft und experimentierte mit Kontrasten. Offen-geschlossen, Licht-Schatten, Festigkeit-Leichtigkeit ... Dieses unmerkliche Spiel mit den Gegensätzen organisiert den Raum sowohl innen als auch außen. In einigen Räumen regiert eine kalte, transparente Atmosphäre und in anderen die Wärme des Holzes und das Spiel mit einzelnen Farben. Die nüchtern dekorierten Räume werden nach ihrer Funktion und der notwendigen Intimität organisiert. So befinden sich die gemeinsam genutzten Räume unten und die intimeren Räume oben.

Craven Residence

Architect: **Frank Fitzgibbons** Photos: © **Julie Phipps**

257

Trois étages forment la structure de ce bâtiment. L'architecte Frank Fitzgibbons maîtrise l'art de combiner le passé, le présent et le future en expérimentant avec les contrastes. Ouvert et fermé, ombre et lumière, légèreté et solidité... Ce jeu subtil avec les contraires, réglemente aussi bien l'intérieur que l'extérieur. Dans certaines pièces il y a une atmosphère froide et transparente, dans d'autres un ambience chaleureuse dûe au bois et au jeu de couleurs particulières. Les chambres sont décorées sobrement et sont disposées selon leur fonction et l'intimité requise. Celles qui sont destinées à l'usage commun sont en bas et les plus privées en haut.

Tres plantas desarrolladas tectónicamente estructuran esta casa. Moviéndose entre el pasado, presente y futuro, el gran acierto del arquitecto Frank Fitzgibbons fue jugar con los contrastes: abierto-cerrado, luz-sombra, solidez-ligereza... Este juego de oposiciones organiza tanto el exterior como los interiores, dominados en algunas estancias por una atmósfera fría y transparente y, en otras, por la calidez de la madera y los juegos cromáticos. Los espacios se organizan a partir de su función y el grado de intimidad que requieren, por lo que las zonas comunes se ubican en los niveles inferiores y las que precisan de más intimidad en la planta superior.

Nothing is banal in this residence, where eclecticism and a stylistic mixture are its strongest features. Despite the geometry of the structure and its discreet appearance, the home lies in a privileged position, where equal parts of both imagination and simplicity form its charm. If the exterior possesses a striking rationalism, the interiors are defined by a well-devised combination of tendencies: an amalgamation of styles that fit together perfectly to form some charming and warm rooms. The result is a home full of personality that is well above fleeting architectural trends.

An diesem Wohnhaus ist nichts banal, Eklektizismus und Vermischung zeichnen es aus. Trotz der Geometrie der architektonischen Struktur und seines diskreten Aussehens handelt es sich um ein besonderes Gebäude in einer wundervollen Umgebung, in dem der Zauber der Einfachheit mit dem der Vorstellungskraft vereint wurde. Von außen betrachtet wirkt es rationell und einfach, und innen wurde durch eine meisterhafte Kombination von Tendenzen ein Gemisch von Stilen geschaffen, die perfekt miteinander kombiniert sind, und warme, behagliche Räume entsehen ließen. Das Ergebnis ist ein Haus mit betontem Eigencharakter, das zeitlos den Modetendenzen widersteht.

Los Angeles House

Architect: **Rubén Ojeda**   Photos: © **Jordi Miralles**

263

Rien n'est banal dans cette maison. Elle se distingue par son éclectisme et son mélange. Malgré la géométrie de sa structure architecturale et son apparence discrète, il s'agit d'une construction très particulière située dans un cadre magnifique, dans lequel la magie de la simplicité et celle de la fantaisie ne font qu'un. Vue du dehors, elle semble simple et rationelle. A l'intérieur on y trouve un mélange parfait de tendances et de styles harmonieusement combinés entre eux créant des pièces chaleureuses et agréables. Le résultat est une maison d'un caractère très particulier pouvant résister aux tendences de la mode.

Nada es banal en esta vivienda que convierte el eclecticismo y el mestizaje en sus mejores armas. A pesar de la geometría de su estructura arquitectónica y de su apariencia discreta, se trata de un espacio privilegiado por su entorno, lleno de soluciones que aúnan a partes iguales el encanto de la sencillez con la imaginación. Si los exteriores se muestran racionalistas y contundentes, los interiores vienen definidos por una sabia combinación de tendencias; una amalgama de estilos perfectamente encajados que configuran unas estancias acogedoras y cálidas. El resultado es una vivienda llena de personalidad que está por encima de la tiranía de las modas pasajeras.

The parking area was the only space kept of the original construction and the rest of the home was completely remodelled on an 'L' shape. The two bodies that make up the structure create an attractive play on volumes, lending the project a suggestive rhythm that is accentuated by the tonality of the façade. If the complex geometry of the residence is one of its star features, the other is colour. Its fresh and daring chromatic combinations limit and define each individual space, heighten its contrasts and act as a backdrop for an interior as personal as it is suggestive, featuring well-known pieces of contemporary design.

Nur der Parkplatz blieb so erhalten, wie er einst war, der Rest des Gebäudes wurde vollständig in L-Form umgebaut. Die beiden Körper dieser Struktur schaffen ein interessantes Formenspiel, was dem Bau eine ansprechende Rhythmik gibt, die durch die Töne der Fassade unterstrichen wird. Die beiden wichtigsten Elemente des Hauses sind also seine komplexe Geometrie und die Farben. Die frischen Farbkombinationen definieren und begrenzen die Räume, heben Kontraste hervor und bilden den Hintergrund für die sehr persönlich gestalteten Innenräume voller wertvoller Beispiele des zeitgenössischen Designs.

Rosenthal House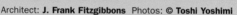

Architect: **J. Frank Fitzgibbons** Photos: © **Toshi Yoshimi**

Seule la place de parque a subsisté à ce qu'il y avait au départ. Le reste de cet immeuble fût complètement transformé en forme de « L ». Les deux parties de cette structure, créent un jeu de formes intéressantes qui donnent un certain rythme à la construction, ce qui vient encore relevé par la couleur des façades. Les deux éléments principaux en sont donc, sa géométrie complexe et les couleurs. Leur combinaison rafraîchissante délimite et définit les différents espaces, font ressortir les contrastes et sont la toile de fond de ces pièces conçues avec beaucoup de personnalité. Elles sont un exemple précieux du design contemporain.

El aparcamiento fue lo único que se respetó de la construcción preexistente; el resto de la vivienda se remodeló por completo. Los dos cuerpos que forman su estructura configuran un juego de volúmenes rotados que otorgan a la construcción un sugerente ritmo acentuado por las tonalidades de la fachada. Si la compleja geometría de la vivienda es uno de los protagonistas indiscutibles, el otro es el color. Las frescas combinaciones cromáticas se encargan de definir y limitar espacios, acentuar los contrastes y ser el telón de fondo de unos interiores muy sugestivos que se han decorado con reconocidas piezas de diseño contemporáneo.

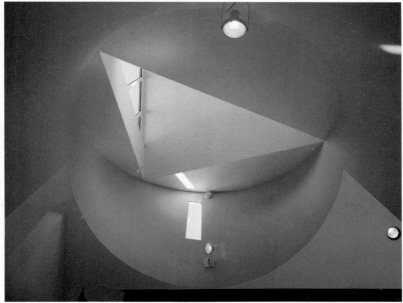

The topography of this home's location called for a project based on different vertical levels. The unusual and almost theatrical entrance is a preview to an interior full of visual richness and an eclecticism in which elegance rules. Strongly defined and pure architectural lines in the rationalist tradition give shape to an ideal stage for an imaginative experiment in combining different styles and tendencies. An evocative balance that manages to create some wonderfully welcoming and functional living areas that, as well as being full of personality, only serve to make the lives of its inhabitants more comfortable.

Die topographischen Bedingungen bestimmten dieses Gebäude, das auf verschiedenen Ebenen in vertikaler Richtung konstruiert wurde. Ein einzigartiger und theatralischer Eingang führt zu einem visuell sehr reichen, eklektischen Raum, der sehr elegant wirkt. Rationelle, architektonische Linien, rein und perfekt definiert, bilden den idealen Schauplatz, um mit der Vermischung, der Kombination von Trends und Stilen und der Phantasie zu experimentieren. Ein ansprechendes Gleichgewicht, aus dem behagliche, funktionelle und sehr persönliche Räume entstehen, die das Leben in ihnen leichter machen.

Pasadena House

Architect: **Rubén Ojeda** Photos: **© Jordi Miralles**

La topographie fût une condition déterminante pour la construction de cette maison, qui fût érigée à la verticale sur plusieurs niveaux. Une entrée très particulière et théâtrale s'ouvre sur une pièce riche et éclectique d'une grande élégance. Des lignes architecturales rationnelles, pures et parfaitement définies, en font un endroit parfait pour expérimenter avec diverses combinaisons de tendances, de styles et de fantaisies. On y trouve un équilibre attrayant duquel naissent des pièces agréables, fonctionnelles et très personnalisées dans lesquelles on se sent immédiatement à l'aise.

Las condiciones topográficas condicionaron que el programa se desarrollara en diferentes niveles en sentido vertical. Una singular y teatral entrada es el preámbulo a un espacio lleno de riqueza visual y eclecticismo en el que impera la ley de la elegancia. Líneas arquitectónicas racionalistas, depuradas y bien definidas, dan forma al escenario ideal en el que experimentar con el mestizaje, la combinación de tendencias y estilos y la imaginación. Un sugerente equilibrio que consigue dibujar unas estancias acogedoras, funcionales y llenas de personalidad al servicio la vida que en ellas desarrollan sus habitantes.

From the onset this home was designed with a profound respect for the environment and the countryside where it is located, making it the project's star feature. It was conceived as a hide-away, full of a personality and charm that incorporates marked simplicity and naturalness. An exquisite, accurate and confined choice of materials, textures and tones achieves a series of suggestive and welcoming interiors that are masterfully worked out. The exterior (that also forms part of the decoration as it can be viewed from the interior) only adds to the serenity and calm that this home radiates.

Die Planung dieses Wohnhauses respektierte die Umgebung und die Landschaft aufs Höchste, die Landschaft nimmt teil und wird zum Hauptdarsteller. Dieses Haus wurde als eine bezaubernde Zuflucht voller Eigencharakter geplant, dessen wichtigste Verbündete die Einfachheit und die Natürlichkeit sind. Durch eine sorgfältige, treffsichere und beschränkte Auswahl an Materialien, Texturen und Tönen wurden behagliche und einladende Räume geschaffen, die meisterhaft gestaltet sind. Der äußere Raum, der Teil der Dekoration ist, die man von innen betrachten kann, verstärkt die Ruhe und Gelassenheit, die das Haus ausstrahlt.

Katzenstein Residence

Architect: **A. Quincy Jones** Photos: © **Benny Chan**

Cette maison fût conçue dès le début avec un profond respect de l'environnement et du paysage où elle se trouve, en faisant les protagonistes. Elle fût envisagée comme un refuge plein de charme et de personnalité, faisant du calme et du naturel ses meilleurs alliés. Un choix réduit mais précis de matériaux, de textures et de couleurs achèvent l'aménagement d'un intérieur engageant et accueillant avec une grande maîtrise. L'extérieur, faisant également partie de la décoration, du fait qu'il est permit de le contempler de l'intérieur, ne fait qu'ajouter au calme et à la sérénité que cette habitation dégage.

La proyección de esta vivienda respeta profundamente el entorno y el paisaje que la envuelve, participando de él y convirtiéndolo en protagonista. La construcción se ha concebido como un refugio lleno de encanto y personalidad que convierte la sencillez y la naturalidad en sus mejores aliados. Una exquisita, atinada y reducida elección de materiales, texturas y tonalidades consiguen configurar unos espacios sugerentes y acogedores que se resuelven con maestría. El exterior, que participa también de la decoración al permitir contemplarlo desde el interior, no hace más que potenciar el sosiego y serenidad que respira la vivienda.

Like most historic residences in L.A., this home was originally built without a garage. So an annexe was built, which as well as solving their parking solution gave the owners a new studio, a guest room and terrace. The new structure is divided into four levels (one for each function) and is connected to the original buidling on the studio level. The minimal palette of materials employed in the exterior magnifies the simplicity of the building's formal structure. This austerity is also seen in its minimalist interior that only serves to accentuate the beauty of the homes dimensions.

Wie die meisten historischen Wohnhäuser verfügte auch dieses ursprünglich nicht über eine Garage. Dieses Problem wurde durch einen Anbau gelöst, in dem sich außer der Garage ein Atelier, ein Gästezimmer und eine Terrasse befinden. Der neue Bau wurde auf vier Ebenen angelegt, eine für jeden neuen Raum. Die Ebene des Ateliers stellt die Verbindung des neuen Anbaus mit dem Hauptgebäude her. Es wurden außen nur wenig verschiedene Materialien benutzt, was die Einfachheit der Form der Strukturen noch verstärkt. Diese Nüchternheit wird in den minimalistischen Räumen im Inneren, welche die Schönheit der Natur der Umgebung betonen, beibehalten.

Guttentag Studio

299

Architect: **Marmol-Radziner + Associates** Photos: © Ricardo Labougle

Comme pour la majorité des anciennes maisons, elle n'avait pas de garage à l'origine. Ce problème fût résolu par la construction d'une annexe dans laquelle on trouve en plus du garage, un atelier, une chambre d'amis et une terrasse. La nouvelle construction fût réalisée sur quatre niveaux ; un pour chaque nouvelle pièce. Le niveau où se trouve l'atelier établi également la liaison avec le bâtiment principal. A l'extérieur, on utilisat peu de matériaux différents ce qui accroît encore la simplicité des formes et des structures. On conserve cette sobriété par un minimalisme intérieur qui est mis en valeur par la beauté de la nature environnante.

Como la mayoría de residencias históricas, esta vivienda originalmente no disponía de garaje. La carencia de aparcamiento se solucionó añadiendo un anexo en el que además se ganó un estudio, una habitación de invitados y una terraza. La nueva estructura queda definida en cuatro niveles –uno por cada nueva estancia– y es la zona destinada a estudio el espacio que se encarga de conectar el nuevo volumen a la construcción principal. La escasa paleta de materiales empleada en el exterior potencia la simplicidad de las estructuras formales, austeridad que se mantiene en unos interiores sobrios que acentúan toda la belleza natural del espacio.

This home occupies a privileged position on the border of a residential area and the countryside. Its divided topography was taken full advantage of when the home was being designed. The construction's occupies two distinct heights, therefore one of the façades hang over a cliff face and the other the lower area. The characteristics of the land also called of a horizontal structure, which was then divided into different levels. A gen-erous, open and transparent central interior acts as the home's axis and main communication point, from which the rest of the rooms can be accessed.

Dieses Wohnhaus liegt dort, wo die Stadt endet und die Natur beginnt. Dieser topographische Kontext wurde auch bei der Planung des Hauses miteinbezogen. Das Gebäude hat zwei Fassaden, eine liegt über einem Abgrund und die andere zeigt auf ein flacheres Gebiet. Aufgrund dieser Besonderheiten des Grundstücks musste das Gebäude horizontal organisiert und in verschiedene Ebenen unterteilt werden. Ein zentraler, großzügiger, offener und fast transparenter Raum wird zum Rückgrat, von dem aus das Haus aufgeteilt wird und das die Verbindung zwischen den verschiedenen Höhen herstellt.

Naiditch Residence

Architect: **Dean Nota Architect, AIA** Photos: © **Erhard Pfeiffer**

311

Cette maison est aux confins de la ville, là où la nature commence. Ce contexte topographique fût pris en considération lors de la construction. Cet immeuble a deux façades. L'une d'elle surplombe un précipice et l'autre donne sur la rase campagne. A cause des particularités du terrain, cette maison fût conçue sur un plan horizontal subdivisé à des degrés de hauteur différents. Une pièce centrale, généreuse, ouverte et transparente en est le pilier principal, duquel partent les autres espaces créant le lien entre les différents niveaux.

Esta edificación se sitúa en esa privilegiada frontera en la que nace la naturaleza y acaban las zonas urbanizadas. Dentro de este contexto topográfico, que se ha aprovechado a la hora de proyectar la vivienda, la construcción se halla entre dos espacios diferenciados. Una de las fachadas se cuelga sobre un precipicio y la otra está en una zona más plana. Las particularidades del terreno obligan a que el programa se organice en horizontal y se divida en niveles. Un generoso espacio central abierto y diáfano se convierte en el eje vertebrador desde el que se organiza la casa y el nexo de unión que comunica con todas las alturas.

Location plan

Axonometric perspective

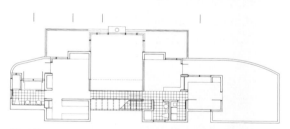

First floor

Ground floor

Frank O. Gehry allowed a total freedom of movement when designing this home, also marked by its unusual location and surprising choice of materials. The absence of any outstanding topographical characteristics afforded the architect an imaginative and technical carte blanche. The result is a construction of unusual morphology that is based in freestanding structures, in which all individual elements mould into one, distinguished entity. The architect has managed to create a dialogue in which, like a jigsaw puzzle, every piece fits perfectly into place.

Frank O. Gehry genoss absolute Freiheit für den Entwurf dieses aufgrund der Gestaltung und der Materialauswahl atypischen Hauses. Da das Grundstück keine besonderen Eigenheiten aufwies, konnte der Architekt seinem Können und seiner Vorstellungskraft freien Lauf lassen. Das Ergebnis ist ein Gebäude mit einer unüblichen From, dessen architektonisches Konzept sich auf unabhängige Strukturen stützt, so dass jedes Element, das Teil des Ganzen ist, eine differenzierte Einheit bildet. Es entstand ein Dialog, in dem sich wie bei einem Puzzle jedes Teil perfekt einpasste.

Schnabel House

Architect: **Frank O. Gehry**

321

Frank O. Gehry a jouit d'une liberté absolue pour ce projet. Cette maison est atypique de par son agencement et le choix des matériaux. Le terrain n'ayant pas de particularités, l'architecte pût laisser libre cour à son savoir et à son imagination. Le résultat en est un bâtiment de forme inhabituelle, d'un concept architectural basé sur des structures indépendentes, ce qui fait que chaque élément tout en faisant partie de tout est une unité en soit. Il en résulte un dialogue permettant, comme dans un puzzle, à chaque pièce de prendre sa place.

Frank O. Gehry dispuso de total libertad de movimientos a la hora de proyectar esta vivienda atípica tanto por su tipología como por la elección de materiales. La ausencia de características topográficas destacables que condicionaran el proyecto permitió que el arquitecto diera rienda suelta a su maestría. El resultado fue una construcción de inusual morfología cuyo planteamiento arquitectónico se basa en estructuras independientes de manera que cada uno de los elementos que conforman el todo es tratado como una entidad diferenciada. Esto crea un sugerente diálogo en el que, como si de un puzzle se tratara, cada una de las piezas encaja perfectamente.

322

Enclosed by some eclectic architectural volumes and situated in one of the most densely populated areas of the western coastal region of metropolitan Los Angeles, this home bares a rational geometry and striking presence. The topographical conditions of its plot and surrounding area called for a vertical project, which in turn created a spatial organisation of different levels. These elements ultimately determined its formal structure and the necessities of it inhabitants, who wanted their home to include a studio and office, influenced the layout of its living areas.

Dieses von eklektischen Gebäuden umgebene Haus in einem der am dichtesten besiedelten Viertel an der Westküste des Stadtgebiets von L.A. zeichnet sich durch seine rationelle Geometrie und überzeugende Präsenz aus. Aufgrund der existierenden Bauvorschriften und des Viertels, in dem das Gebäude liegt, musste es vertikal angelegt werden. Da nach oben gebaut wurde, hat der Architekt auch den Raum auf verschiedenen Ebenen aufgeteilt. Die Lage bestimmt seine formelle Struktur, und die Notwendigkeiten der Bewohner, die ein Atelier zum Malen und ein privates Büro brauchten, beeinflussten die Aufteilung der Räume.

Bergman Residence

Architect: **Dean Nota Architect, AIA** Photos: © **Erhard Pfeiffer**

325

Cette maison entourée de bâtiments éclectiques est dans l'un des quartiers les plus peuplé de la côte ouest de L.A. Elle se caractérise de par sa géométrie rationelle et une présence très convainquante. A cause de la réglementation sur les constructions et du quartier où elle se trouve, elle fût construite à la verticale. Etant construite en hauteur, les pièces sont réparties sur plusieurs niveaux. Sa situation détermine les formes de sa structure et ses habitants, qui nécessitaient un atelier de peinture et un bureau, décidèrent de l'agencement intérieur.

Rodeada de eclécticos volúmenes arquitectónicos y situada en una de las zonas más densamente pobladas de la costa oeste del área metropolitana de Los Ángeles, esta casa es una edificación de racional geometría y contundente presencia. La normativa, las condiciones de la zona y su enclave obligaban a que el programa se desarrollara en vertical. El crecer hacia arriba imponía, también, una organización espacial en diferentes niveles. La ubicación determinó su estructura formal y la necesidad de los habitantes –que deseaban que la vivienda incluyera un estudio de pintura y un despacho privado– influyó en la distribución y articulación de las estancias.

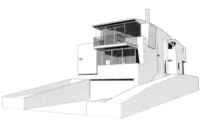

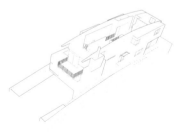

Axonometrics perspectives

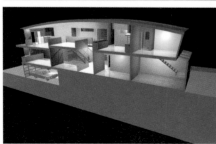
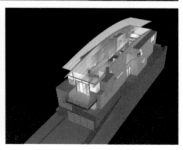

Located in the quiet residential areas in the West of Los Angeles, this house, designed by its owner Ron Rezek in the fifties, was created as a family home with the characteristics of an art gallery. It is a simple construction, based on a rectangular floor and a semicircular volume. The latter attached at one side to the main entrance acts as the home's counterpoint by breaking its dominant angles and straight lines. The architecture effortlessly integrates into its surroundings, permitting the interior spaces to open up to the exterior and letting in a natural light accompanied by some spectacular views.

Dieses von seinem Eigentümer Ron Rezek in den fünfziger Jahren entworfene Haus liegt in einem ruhigen Wohngebiet im Westen von L.A. Er wollte ein Familienwohnhaus mit den Eigenschaften einer Kunstgalerie schaffen. Auf einem einfachen, rechteckigen Grundriss erhebt sich neben dem Haupteingang ein halbrunder Körper, der den Kontrapunkt bildet, welcher die dominierenden Winkel und geraden Linien bricht. Die Architektur fügt sich auf natürliche Weise in die Landschaft ein, so dass sich die Innenräume nach außen öffnen, von Licht überflutet werden und einen wundervollen Ausblick bieten.

Rezek House

Architect: **Michael W. Folonis** Photos: © **Julie Phipps**

Cette maison conçue dans les années cinquante par son propriétaire Ron Rezek, est située dans l'un des quartiers calmes de L.A. Il voulût créer un habitation familiale ayant un caractère de galerie d'art. Partant d'un plan rectangulaire, une construction arrondie s'élève à coté de l'entrée principale créant ainsi un contraste en brisant les angles dominants et les lignes droites. L'architecture s'adapte de façon très naturelle au paysage. Les pièces qui s'ouvrent sur l'extérieur sont inondées de lumière et offrent une vue magnifique.

Ubicada en una área residencial al oeste de Los Ángeles, la casa fue proyectada por su propietario, Ron Rezek, en los años 50, con la idea de crear una casa familiar que dispusiera de las características propias de una galería de arte. Parte de un planteamiento de edificación sencillo: planta rectangular en la que destaca un cuerpo semicircular –el contrapunto que rompe con los ángulos y las líneas rectas dominantes– anexo a un lado de la entrada principal. La arquitectura se integra en el paisaje de manera natural permitiendo que los espacios interiores se abran al exterior, queden invadidos por la luz y gocen de espectaculares vistas.

The owners of this residence needed a project to replace their old home after it had been destroyed in a fire. The new structure had to adjust to the necessities of a couple and their child and also had to incorporate a large library and a space for a grande piano. Situated on a hill in the north of Los Angeles, surrounded by other homes and fixed by the limits of an adjacent swimming pool, the architect had to adapt to these and various other restrictions when calculating the dimensions of the home. The main floor and mezzanine were used as a starting point, with the other rooms distributed according to their function.

Die Eigentümer, deren ehemaliges Haus durch einen Brand zerstört wurde, brauchten ein neues Zuhause. Dieses neue Gebäude sollte sich an die Notwendigkeiten eines Paares mit einem Kind anpassen, und eine Bibliothek und einen Raum für das große Piano haben. Das Haus liegt auf einem Hügel im Norden von L.A. und ist von anderen Häusern umgeben. Der Architekt musste sich bei der Planung an den daneben liegenden Swimmingpool und andere Faktoren anpassen. Das Haus besitzt ein Hauptstockwerk und ein Zwischengeschoss, und die Räume sind ihrer Funktion entsprechend verteilt.

Poloynis Residence

Architect: **Dean Nota Architect, AIA**   Photos: © **Erhard Pfeiffer**

Les propriétaires de cette résidence désiraient remplacer leur ancienne maison détruite par un incendie. Les nouvelles structures devaient tenir compte des nécessités d'un couple et de leur fils qui désirait disposer en plus, d'une grande bibliothèque et d'un emplacement destiné à un grand piano. Située sur une coline au nord de L.A., entourée d'autres habitations et délimitée par une piscine adjacente, l'architecte dû tenir compte de cela ainsi que d'autres restrictions en calculant les dimensions de cette nouvelle demeure. Mezzanine et niveau principal en sont le centre d'où partent les autres pièces, réparties selon leurs fonctions.

Los propietarios requerían un programa residencial que reemplazara su antiguo hogar, destruido tras un incendio. Esta nueva estructura debía acomodarse a las necesidades de una pareja con un hijo, debía disponer de una gran biblioteca y de una zona en la que ubicar un gran piano. Situada sobre una colina al norte de Los Ángeles, rodeada de otras viviendas, delimitada por una piscina adyacente y con una serie de condiciones a cumplir, el arquitecto se adaptó a todos estos condicionantes a la hora de proyectar los volúmenes de la casa. El programa se organiza en un nivel principal y un entrepiso y las estancias se distribuyen a partir de la función que se les otorga.

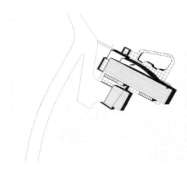

Location plan

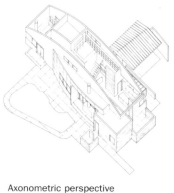

Axonometric perspective

Floor

Richard Neutra formed part of a new era of North America architecture. He was firmly of the belief that context, as well as determining the type of structure to be built, was enormously important in influencing the conduct of human behaviour. His constructions are noted for their functionalism and the visual sharpness of their forms. This exquisite simplicity of volumes is extremely evident in the Singleton House, built in 1959. A striking, decidedly modern work in which its environment gains special importance by isolating and protecting the work and at the same time highlighting its extremely defined profile.

Richard Neutra war der Vorreiter einer neuen Ära der nordamerikanischen Architektur. Er war fest davon überzeugt, dass der Kontext nicht nur die Art der Konstruktion bestimmt, sondern dass er auch das Benehmen der Menschen beeinflusst. Seine Bauten sind funktionell und ihre Form von großer, visueller Reinheit. Diese erlesene Einfachheit der Formen fällt insbesondere an dem 1959 gebauten Singleton-Haus auf. Ein überzeugendes Bauwerk sehr moderner Prägung, in dem die Umgebung eine ganz besondere Bedeutung gewinnt, denn sie isoliert und beschützt das Haus, hebt gleichzeitig dessen definiertes Profil hervor und macht es einzigartig.

Singleton House

Architect: **Richard Neutra** Photos: © **Ricardo Labougle**

345

Richard Neutra fût l'un des précurseurs d'une ère nouvelle de l'architecture américaine. Il était convaincu que l'environnement non seulement détermine le genre de la construction, mais qu'il influence aussi le comportement des êtres humains. Ses maisons sont fonctionnelles et leurs formes sont d'une grande pureté. On le remarque particulièrement dans la simplicité noble des formes de la « Singleton House », qui fût construite en 1959. Un édifice convainquant et d'un caractère moderne, où l'environnement a une signification importante, car il isole et protège la maison tout en définissant et soulignant son profile, la rendant ainsi exceptionnelle.

Richard Neutra inauguró una nueva era en la arquitectura norteamericana. Estaba firmemente convencido de que el contexto, además de determinar el tipo de construcción que en él debía proyectarse, adquiría una enorme importancia al influir en el comportamiento de las personas. Sus construcciones se rigen por la funcionalidad y la nitidez visual de las formas. Esa exquisita simplicidad de volúmenes destaca en la casa Singleton, edificada en 1959. Una contundente obra decididamente moderna en la que el entorno cobra una singular relevancia ya que aísla y protege la vivienda a la vez que la individualiza y hace destacar su definido perfil.

The tension that provokes the upright nature of this home's geometric lines dissolves with the soft, rounded lines of the façade. Although architects Mark Cigolle and Kim Coleman were allowed a certain dose of artistic license, they did not let it interfere with functionality of the project. Almost as if it were a theatre set and the inhabitants the actors, they have designed a home full of personality. This lesson in architectural design acts as a backdrop for a series of meticulously organised interiors in which stylistic richness is the star player, along with high quality materials and a refined taste.

Die durch die geraden, geometrischen Linien erzeugte Spannung löst sich durch die runden Formen der Fassade auf. Mark Cigolle und Kim Coleman, die für dieses Gebäude verantwortlichen Architekten, erlaubten sich einige stilistische Freiheiten, die jedoch niemals die Funktionalität beeinträchtigen. Es entstanden Räume mit starkem Eigencharakter, so als ob es sich um die Bühne für eine Aufführung handelte. Eine vorbildliche Architektur bildet den Hintergrund für treffsicher organsisierte Räume, die sich durch ihren stilistischen Reichtum, edle Materialien und guten Geschmack auszeichnen.

Cigolle & Coleman House

355

Architect: **Cigolle & Coleman Architects** Photos: © **Undine Pröhl**

La tension produite par les lignes géométriques droites, vient interrompue par les formes arrondies de la façade. Mark Cigolle et Kim Coleman, les architectes responsables de la conception de ce bâtiment, se permettent certaines libertés stylistiques sans porter préjudice à son fonctionnalisme. Le résultat sont des pièces ayant un caractère très marqué tout comme si il s'agissait de scènes de théâtre. Une architecture exemplaire qui crée la toile de fond de ces espaces agencés de façon parfaite. Elles se distinguent par leur richesse de style, des matériaux nobles et un bon goût certain.

La tensión que provoca la rectitud de las líneas geométricas se diluye con la suavidad de los trazos contorneados que se incorporan a la fachada. Mark Cigolle y Kim Coleman, arquitectos encargados de proyectar la vivienda, se conceden algunas licencias estilísticas que en ningún momento interfieren en la funcionalidad de ésta. Como si de la escenografía de una representación teatral se tratara, se ha creado un espacio lleno de personalidad. Todo un ejercicio de arquitectura que es el telón de fondo de unos interiores organizados con destreza y en los que destaca la riqueza estilística, el empleo de materiales nobles y el buen gusto.

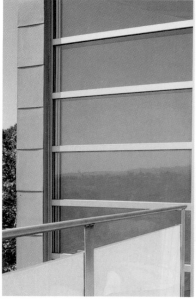

Architectural coherency defines this residence located by the sea. The specific relation that exists between the two defined volumes of its façade and its surroundings (predominated by the horizon and the contrast of sea-sky and sea-earth) also mark its geometric layout. Straight lines reign in this construction in which details have been given careful attention, especially in the blending of materials, textures and tones to achieve the desired affect. The result is a striking home in which open, light and airy spaces dominate.

Der architektonische Zusammenhang definiert dieses Haus am Meer. Die spezifische Beziehung zwischen den definierten Formen der Fassade und des Grundstücks, auf dem die Linien des Horizontes und die Gegensätze zwischen Land-Himmel und Land-Meer vorherrschen, bestimmt auch seine geometrischen Linien. Gerade Linien dominieren, Details wurden sehr sorgfältig ausgearbeitet und besonderen Wert legten die Planer auf die akzentuierte Auswahl von Materialien, Texturen und Tönen, um die gewünschte Wirkung zu erreichen. Das Ergebnis ist ein beeindruckendes Gebäude, in dem die offenen, hellen und großzügigen Räume vorherrschen.

Kelly Residence

Architect: **Lorcan O'Herlihy Architects** Photos: © **Eric Staudermaier**

363

La cohérence architecturale définit cette maison du bord de mer. Les relations spécifiques entre les formes définies de la façade et du terrain sur lesquelles prédominent les lignes de l'horizon et les contrastes entre terre et ciel, et terre et mer, déterminent également ses lignes géométriques. Les lignes droites dominent. Les détails ont été soigneusement étudiés et les constructeurs ont donné beaucoup d'importance au choix des matériaux, des textures et des couleurs afin d'obtenir les effets voulu. Le résultat est un bâtiment imposant, dans lequel prédominent de grandes pièces claires et ouvertes.

La coherencia arquitectónica define a esta vivienda situada frente al mar. La específica relación existente entre los definidos volúmenes de su fachada y el enclave en el que se ubica (predominio de la línea del horizonte, contrastes tierra-cielo, tierra-mar) marcan también sus geométricos trazos. Las líneas rectas imperan en esta construcción en la que se han cuidado al máximo los detalles y se ha puesto especial empeño en conjugar de manera acertada la paleta de materiales, texturas y tonalidades para lograr el efecto deseado. El resultado es una casa de presencia contundente en la dominan los espacios abiertos, iluminados y generosos.

The natural surroundings and the topography of this home-studio's immediate area were the key, but not the only, factors the Japanese architect Arata Isozaki, had to keep in mind when he sat down at the drawing board. At the expressed wish of the home's proprietor, also an art collector, he constructed an enclosure of giant, transparent spaces laid out in harmonious proportions and inundated with natural light. The rectangular structure consists of two floors and is divided into three cubic bodies. Four isosceles triangles, built in copper and open on the diagonal to the roof, give form to the skylights.

Die Berücksichtigung der umgebenden Natur und der Typologie der Zone, in der dieses Haus/Atelier errichtet wurde, sind nur zwei der Faktoren, die für den japanischen Architekten bei der Planung ausschlaggebend waren. Isozaki baute auf ausdrücklichen Wunsch der Hausherrin, die eine große Kunstliebhaberin ist, große, durchscheinende Räume mit harmonischen Proportionen, die vom Tageslicht überflutet werden. Der rechteckige Grundriss erstreckt sich über zwei Stockwerke und unterteilt sich in drei kubische Körper. Vier gleichschenklige Dreiecke aus Kupfer, die sich diagonal auf dem Dach öffnen, bilden die Dachfenster.

Bjornson House

Architect: **Arata Isozaki** Photos: **© Richard Bryant/Arcaid**

L'architecte japonais Isozaki a dû tenir compte principalement de deux facteurs déterminants lorsqu'il a fait les plans de cette maison/atelier. Tout d'abord de la nature environnante et également de la typologie de l'endroit. Isozaki se conforma au désirs formels de la propriétaire qui est une grande amatrice d'art. Il construit des grandes pièces transparentes inondées de lumière ayant des proportions harmonieuses. Le plan rectangulaire s'étend sur deux étages et est divisé en trois parties cubiques. Quatre triangles de cuivre ayant des côté égaux s'ouvrent en diagonale sur le toit constituant les fenêtres.

Considerar el entorno natural y la tipología constructiva de la zona en la que se enclava esta casa-estudio fueron algunos de los factores que el arquitecto tuvo en cuenta a la hora de proyectar la construcción, pero no los únicos. Arata Isozaki, por expreso deseo de la propietaria –muy amante del arte–, construyó un contenedor con grandes espacios diáfanos de proporciones armónicas inundados de luz natural. La estructura, de planta rectangular, se desarrolla en dos pisos y se divide en tres cuerpos cúbicos. Cuatro triángulos isósceles, realizados en cobre y abiertos en diagonal en la cubierta, se encargan de conformar las claraboyas.

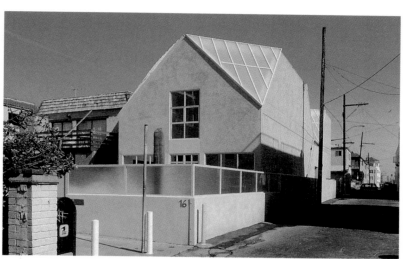

Two powerful, intersecting volumes that jut out between the craggy sandstone terrain. Both bodies have been covered in modular horizontal sheets of pine with which interior light can be graduated through the slats between the pieces of wood. The glass façade establishes an emotive communication between exterior and interior whilst at the same time plays with the concept of visible/invisible through its mobility and translucence. An ingenious lesson in architecture that bares fruit to a construction that takes full advantage of the splendour of its location.

Zwei imposante, rechteckige Körper kreuzen sich und erheben sich über ein abschüssiges Gelände aus Sandstein, auf dem sich dieses Gebäude befindet. Beide Körper besitzen eine horizontal verlaufende, modulare Kiefernholzverkleidung, durch deren Öffnungen sich das Licht ins Gebäudeinnere filtert. Die verglaste Fassade auf einer Seite stellt die Kommunikation zwischen innen und außen her und spielt mit den Konzepten sichtbar und unsichtbar, da sie beweglich und transparent ist. Eine meisterhafte Lektion auf dem Gebiet der Architektur, durch die ein wundervolles Gebäude entstanden ist, das alle Bedingungen des Ortes optimal ausnutzt.

exton McCarthy Residence

Architect: **Lorcan O'Herlihy Architects** Photos: © **Undine Pröhl**

Deux rectangles imposants se croisent et s'élèvent sur ce terrain escarpé plein de grès où se trouve cette construction. Ces deux corps sont revêtus de panneaux en pin placés à l'horizontale entre lesquels la lumière peut s'infiltrer à l'intérieur du bâtiment. La façade, vitrée d'un côté permet la communication entre l'intérieur et l'extérieur jouant sur les plans du visible et de l'invisible du fait de sa mobilité et de sa transparence. Une magnifique leçon d'architecture qui a permit de concevoir une construction pareille en exploitant l'endroit de façon optimale.

Dos poderosos volúmenes rectangulares en intersección sobresalen de entre el escarpado terreno de piedra arenisca en que se enclava esta construcción. Ambos cuerpos se han revestido de una piel horizontal modular de madera de pino; las aberturas que deja la madera permiten graduar la entrada de luz que se filtra en el interior. Por su parte, la fachada acristalada de una de sus caras establece una sugerente comunicación entre interior y exterior a la vez que permite jugar con el concepto de visible e invisible al ser móviles y translúcidos. Una magistral lección de arquitectura que concibe una construcción que despliega todo su esplendor al aprovechar las condiciones del lugar en que se ubica.

If Californian architecture is characterised by eclecticism and a stylistic mix this residence is a good example. Situated on summit of a hill with sweeping views of its surroundings, this home's principal concept is one of minimal lines and reduced form which can also be seen in the materials (stone, wood and glass) used in its austere, unadorned interior. This sparse and simple use of forms, far from becoming a burden, has remained the most memorable feature of this home and is the thing that first strikes you.

Dieses Gebäude ist ein gutes Beispiel für die kalifornische Architektur, die sich durch Vermischung von Stilen und Eklektizismus auszeichnet. Dieses Haus, das sich auf einer Anhöhe befindet, von der aus man einen wundervollen Blick hat, zeichnet sich durch die Minimierung der Linien und formelle Reduktion aus, die sogar an den verwendeten Materialien zu erkennen ist: Stein, Holz und Glas, und eine karge und schlichte Innendekoration. Diese formelle Reduktion und Einfachheit ist jedoch sehr ansprechend, sie ist der interessanteste Aspekt des Gebäudes. Dieses architektonische Konzept überzeugt und gefällt vom ersten Moment an.

Coombs House

Architect: **Goldman Firth Architects** Photos: © **Undine Pröhl**

Cette construction est un bon exemple de l'architecture californienne, qui se distingue par son éclectisme et son mélange de styles. Cette maison se trouve sur une coline, de laquelle on a une vue magnifique. Elle se distingue par un minimum de lignes et une restriction des formes. On le retrouve également dans l'emploi des matériaux utilisés: De la pierre, du bois et du verre, ainsi que dans une décoration intérieure simple et peu abondante. Cette simplicité et ces restrictions, sont pourtant l'aspect intéressant de cette construction. Ce concept architectural peut convaincre et plaire dès le premier instant.

Si la arquitectura californiana se caracteriza por el mestizaje y el eclecticismo, esta vivienda es un buen ejemplo de ello. Situada en la cima de una colina que permite dominar visualmente el entorno, la concepción de esta casa se rige por la minimización de trazos y la reducción formal, que se aprecia incluso en los materiales empleados (piedra, madera y cristal) y en la austera y escueta decoración interior. Esa reducción y simpleza formal tan absoluta, lejos de convertirse en un lastre, se torna en la máxima virtud de esta construcción, que se percibe de forma contundente y directa desde el primer momento.

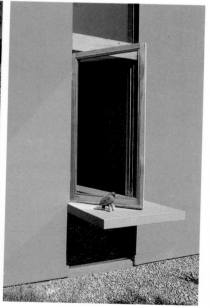

Other Designpocket titles by teNeues:

Berlin Apartments 3-8238-5596-4

Cafés & Restaurants 3-8238-5478-X

Cool Hotels 3-8238-5556-5

Country Hotels 3-8238-5574-3

Exhibition Design 3-8238-5548-4

Furniture/Möbel/Meubles/Mobile Design 3-8238-5575-1

Italian Interior Design 3-8238-5495-X

London Apartments 3-8238-5558-1

New York Apartments 3-8238-5557-3

Office Design 3-8238-5578-6

Paris Apartments 3-8238-5571-9

Product Design 3-8238-5597-2

Showrooms 3-8238-5496-8

Spa & Wellness Hotels 3-8238-5595-6

Staircases 3-8238-5572-7

Tokyo Houses 3-8238-5573-5

Each volume:

12.5 x 18.5 cm
400 pages
c. 450 color illustrations